ॐ

OUR HERITAGE

REVISITED

A glimpse into ancient Indian texts

Anju Saha

"Dharma is not amenable to sense perception and the other means of knowledge" (From "The Purva Mimansa Sutras of Jaimini" by Mahamahopadhyay Ganganatha Jha – 1.1.4)

This book is based on my research on a large number of translated works on our scriptures with the sole purpose of conveying basic facts and ideas to members of Aradhana Satsang, youngsters, friends and relatives. Any commonality of expressions with the consulted works is unintentional.

Grateful thanks to my husband Raghav and my most loved daughter Smiti for their unceasing interest and inputs, and to my nephew Suhit for the invaluable encouragement given.

I am also greatly indebted to Mrs. Usha Gupta (mentor) and the other members of my satsang group for the continued inspiration.

Anju Saha
Email:anjusaha@hotmail.com

© March 2015.
First Edition : 2015, Reprint November 2017.
ISBN 978-93-5235-074-2
₹ 350.

The Whys and Hows of this book

The exercise of writing this book arose out of a simple question by a niece who wanted to know which our Hindu texts were. I have always been a practicing Hindu and after my retirement from the State Bank of India, I have found the time and the inclination to join the Aradhana Satsang group. My interest in the subject of our religion and culture has now deepened. The urge to give an answer in a systematic manner resulted in a hunt that lasted over eighteen months.

And I was fascinated by the profoundness I found in these texts. Imagine maintaining accuracy over what appears to be millions and millions of words, over thousands of years, by sheer memory alone. The precision of our *Panchangs* (calendars with detailed calculations of the movements of cosmic bodies), with such limited tools and without computers, had always rendered me awestruck, but the extent of our knowledge of astrology that I now found in the Vedic times was beyond my imagination.

I knew that the concept of zero came from India; I now learnt that Baudhayan had written the rule of the Pythagoras theorem (though without its proof) that was a few centuries earlier. Then the vast notions of time—from the minutest to the infinite mentioned in the Purans, the beautiful poetry, and the concepts in the Upanishads—the list of my learnings of our past can go on and on.

I saw that most of the works and studies in English available on the Net were by foreigners, rather than Indians. Recently too, Oxford University Press has stated that they have brought out the first complete English translation of the Rig Ved in over a century.

A lot of this knowledge is also available on the sites of universities abroad. I read that efforts have been made to prepare accurate versions of the Mahabharat (available in Pune) and of Valmiki's Ramayan (in Vadodra). And I wish and wish that these efforts really multiply.

The more I read, the more I remained engrossed. I thought—there is so much new that I have learnt about our country's past, before ever so much was destroyed. Maybe there are many others who have some gaps in their knowledge of our great religious past. This finally led to this book. From the very outset I focused on making this a primer, meant for the novice, and not for the large number of our very learned.

I have done considerable reading and have used extensively the contents found. The sources of my guidance are so many, I have lost track, but most information has been crosschecked from more than one source.

I now hope that each one of you who reads this book gets similarly fascinated. And perhaps are inspired to do some further reading on a topic of your interest.

On Sanskrit

It may be realized that the Vedic Sanskrit language of our ancient scriptures – the lexicon, grammar and thought presentation of those times was widely different from the more recent and classical Sanskrit. Today most people do not know even classical Sanskrit, and are diffident about approaching these texts.

We are also trying to understand the Upanishads (and other texts) in today's setting, many millennia after these were composed. This naturally poses an intellectual challenge to discover words, expressions, grammar and language of those days that match our present system of knowledge, perceptions about society, language, meanings of similar words and expressions, means of accessing knowledge etc. This realization demands some patience, tolerance and room for respect, and an open mindedness to take both the basic and the deeper messages.

Our religious texts are written in Sanskrit – Vedic or later. When writing these words in English, the pronunciation is impacted. Unlike Hindi, Sanskrit often has words ending with a *halant*. So a word can have an ending with a *halant*, the full consonant, or the 'aa' *maatra* (depicted as "ā" in English). Typically three different rules are used for indicating these. However, in general writing, the third style is frequently omitted thereby merging the last two pronunciations.

Classical Sanskrit uses about 50 letters (vowels and

consonants). Besides, there is also the concept of half consonants, so there are combinations of two or more consonants leading to a very large number of conjunct consonants.

English, on the other hand, has only 26 letters in the alphabet. In order to represent accurately and unambiguously the sounds of Sanskrit, an agreed system is used - the International Alphabet of Sanskrit Transliteration (IAST). This involves combinations of letters and the usage of several diacritical marks. Both the writer and the reader need to know these rules, which can be quite complicated for the layman. In common writings, the IAST spellings are used but the diacritics are frequently omitted resulting in the pronunciation getting impacted / distorted.

In this book, diacritical marks have not been used, and some English spellings have been linked with the Hindi pronunciation. Where considered necessary the words in Hindi have been given alongside as I feel this makes for easier reading. Many of you may find this awkward initially but do bear with me here.

The Hindi words used in this book are given in italics.

An Introduction to Ancient Hindu Scriptures

Table of Contents
Part I

Part II

आ नो भद्राः क्रतवो यन्तु विश्वतः
(ऋग्वेद: 1-89-i).

Let noble thoughts come to us from all sides.
(Rig Ved: 1-89-i)

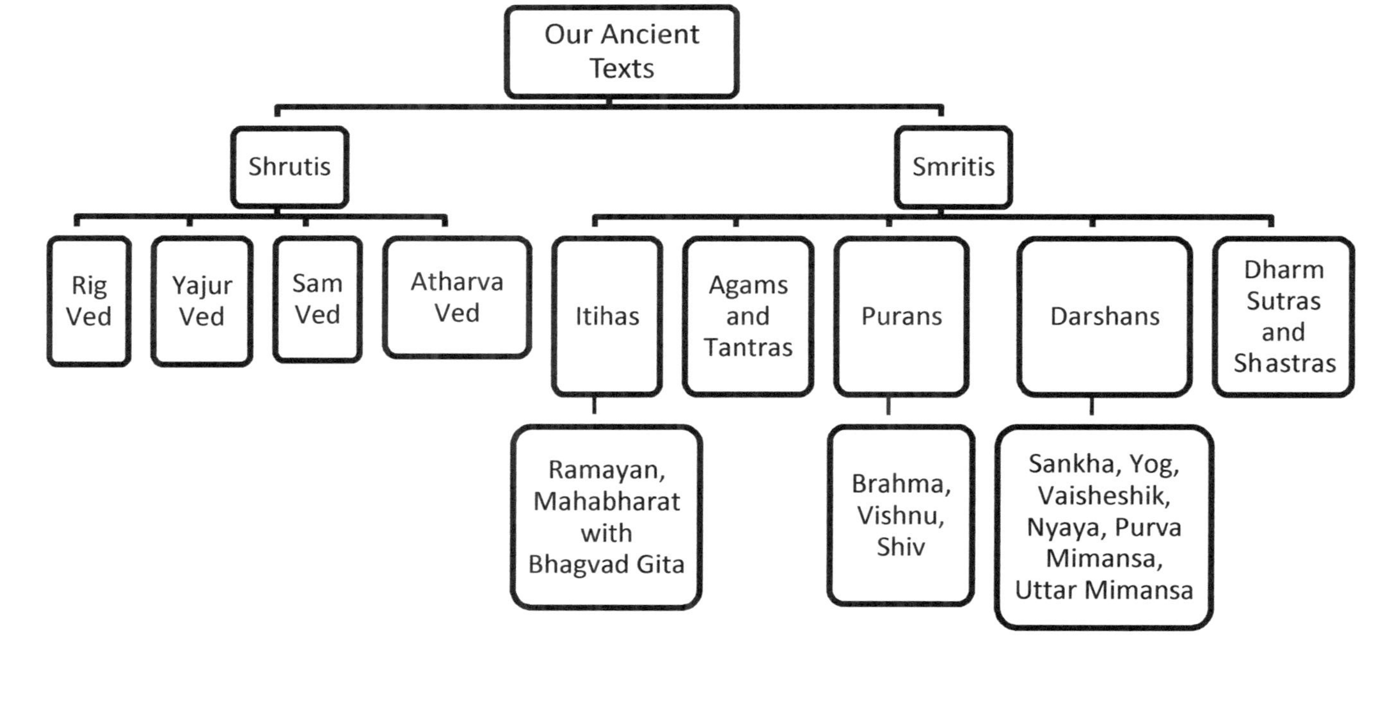

Our Ancient Texts
Shrutis
Smritis
Rig Ved
Yajur Ved
Sam Ved
Atharva Ved
Itihas
Agams and Tantras
Purans
Darshans
Dharm Sutras and Shastras
Ramayan, Mahabharat with Bhagvad Gita
Brahma, Vishnu, Shiv
Sankha, Yog, Vaisheshik, Nyaya, Purva Mimansa, Uttar Mimansa

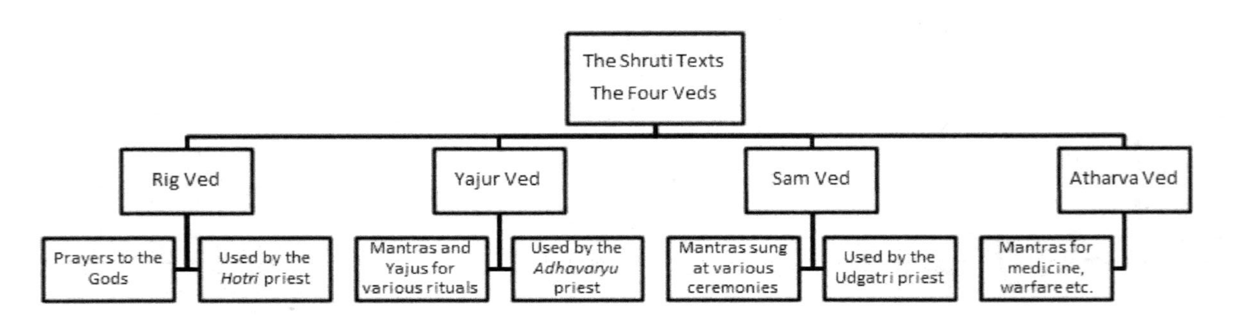

The Shruti Texts
The Four Veds
Rig Ved
Yajur Ved
Sam Ved
Atharva Ved
Prayers to the Gods
Used by the Hotri priest
Mantras and Yajus for various rituals
Used by the Adhavaryu priest
Mantras sung at various ceremonies
Used by the Udgatri priest
Mantras for medicine, warfare etc.

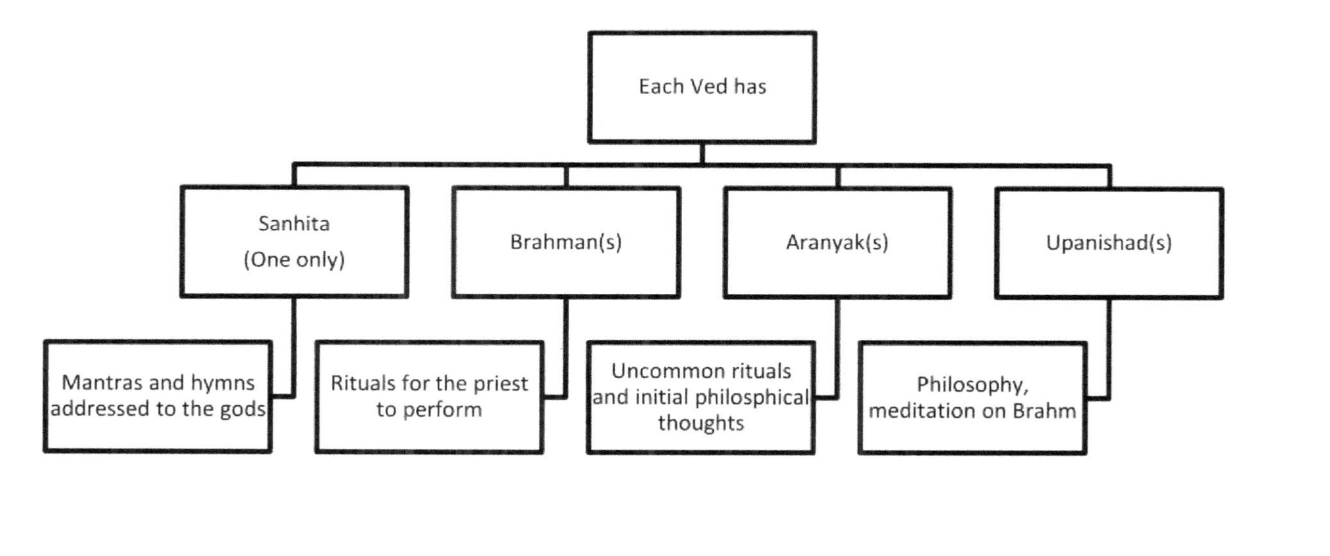

Each Ved has
Sanhita (One only)
Brahman(s)
Aranyak(s)
Upanishad(s)
Mantras and hymns addressed to the gods
Rituals for the priest to perform
Uncommon rituals and initial philosphical thoughts
Philosophy, meditation on Brahm

Other Associated Texts

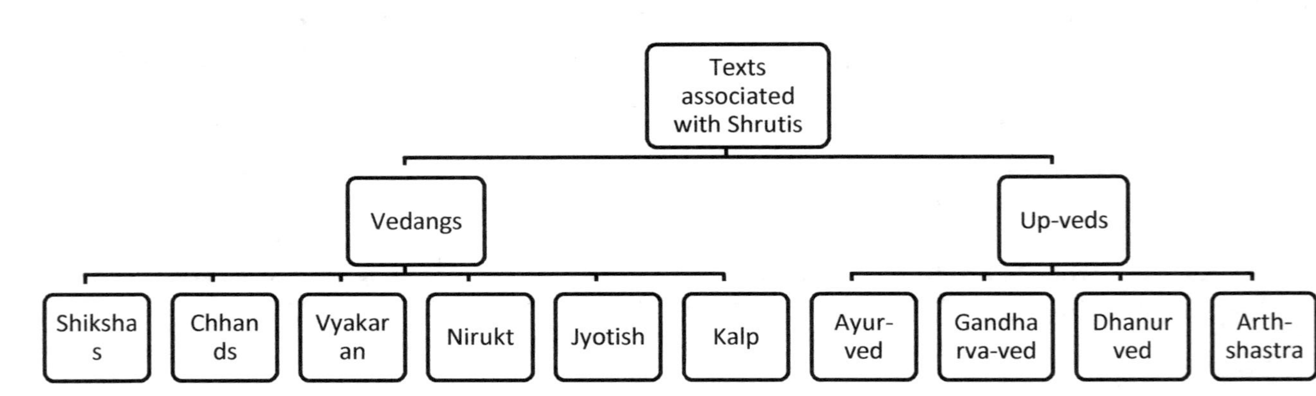

Introduction to the Shruti texts

Background

When asked which are the main religious texts that we Hindus follow, many of us draw a blank. These are not the commonly known Ramayan or Mahabharat which, though great expositions of Hindu religion, are epics or stories, not pure religious texts.

The primary reason for the confusion is that there is a vast multiplicity of thoughts and their resultant scriptures (texts) that have coexisted over centuries, giving rise to the inability or difficulty in mentioning a single or even a limited number of texts describing the Hindu religion and its associated practices and beliefs. Hinduism has emerged as a way of life, a philosophy encompassing varied traditions rather than a set of directives on which our religion is based. Hinduism does have some tenets and pillars but allows for many variations and viewpoints.

No single book leads to the principles of our religion. There are many sacred writings that are sources of Hindu doctrine. Ancient Hindu philosophy is represented in a corpus of texts where the authors and dates of the composition are typically unknown. The earliest knowledge that we have is of deep-thinking philosophers, and their literature is characterized by a deep and constant concern with man's spiritual destiny as manifested by their rich philosophical concepts and the great epic poems written subsequently. Chief among these texts are those collectively known as the Veds (वेद), perhaps the oldest religious texts in the world. They consist mainly of praise / hymns to the gods of Nature as also instructions for the rituals of worship. The latest works within the class of texts known as the Veds, are the Upanishads and these are generally more philosophical. These Indian scriptures very loosely laid the foundation for most of India's philosophical schools.

A beauty of Hindu scriptures is to resolve the complexities associated with Creation in its entirety, including its primeval cause. This led to the evolution of a multiplicity of thoughts and knowledge systems in our religion and the writing of so many books—the Sanhitas, Upanishads, the Purans etc. A similar evolution is also seen across the world of science and literature. In today's science too, we have been struggling with understanding Nature, and the more we try to understand it, the greater is the manifold increase in the complexities. The example of understanding the Big Bang is one; particle after particle being discovered and written about, but we are still far from a unified picture.

Hindu literature goes back many thousands of years and, despite advances in technology, the earliest texts have still defied attempts to actually date them. Hinduism has, perhaps, the unique distinction of being a living faith having such numerous and ancient scriptures, and yet boast of an unbroken tradition so faithfully preserved. Ancient Hindus seldom kept written records of their literary, religious or even political developments and the earliest known knowledge is that which was "heard" by our sages or *rishis* and passed on over generations by word of mouth, these were converted into writings only a very long time later. It is to be appreciated that the knowledge evolved over decades and centuries and had to be preserved until these were captured in writings; this must have been a marathon task.

Documented and oral knowledge have lived together for centuries and our reliance on oral knowledge continues to exist in every important aspect of our life. One can easily appreciate that events took place and that knowledge existed in our country without being written down / recorded when we see how our recipes are faithfully handed down over generations, how our marriages are solemnized - accepted socially and legally without any documentation and held binding over lifetime, and how births and deaths take place without any documentary evidence (till very recently).

There was a vast bank of knowledge that was "heard", as tradition has it, directly from Brahma (ब्रह्मा) the Creator, by his disciples Marichi, Atri, Angira and others whom we know as great *rishis* in Indian philosophy. This was then handed down through centuries orally from teacher to disciple; these are known as the **Shruti** (श्रुति) meaning what was heard (*'shru'* means to hear). They were not written – perhaps because the written script was not developed enough at that time, or even if it was reasonably developed, it was not easy to write down on palm leaves or other material. Or perhaps because it was considered that the written word could be available to all, whereas this sacred knowledge was to be accessible only to those who had acquired it through a qualified teacher, and after years of study.

What one finds is that the earliest texts were large in number, really voluminous and written in Vedic Sanskrit. In order to now understand these texts, one needs to know the language, and be properly trained and equipped with necessary tools and knowledge. And since even the translations are not simple to understand or interpret, even today they are not read by the common man. Little is known about their origin, and their development. The *Shruti* texts comprise mainly the **four *Veds*** (वेद) (the *Rig, Yajur, Sam* and *Athrava Veds*), which are the basic scriptures, as also their attached books. The Veds are also known as the *Shabd Brahma*.

The primary meaning of the word '*Ved*' is knowledge; it also refers to the words in which that knowledge is represented. Hence '*Ved*' denotes not only the early religious and philosophical wisdom of India, but also the books in which that wisdom is preserved. Ved is also not the name of any particular book(s), but of the literature of a particular epoch extending over, say, a few thousand years and hence of a diversified nature.

The earliest texts are estimated to have been written somewhere in the range from 4000 BCE to 1200 BCE (some sources place them much earlier while others hold them to be later), with the first of the Upanishads (the concluding part of the Veds) being placed around 800 BCE.

The *Veds* are not considered 'books' in the typical sense, as they require the human person to vocalize the innumerable nuances and fine stresses without which they are robbed of their essence. The four *Veds– Rig, Yajur, Sam,* and *Atharva –* are also not the work of any single *rishi.* In ancient India, there were many *rishis* such as Angira, Bhrigu, Yagyavalkya, and Gargi (a woman), living simple lives, meditating in the Himalayas and along the banks of rivers. Their intense contemplation was on the basic fundamentals of life – the cause of birth, the essentials of life and living, and on this world. It is said that they received God's blessings, that God revealed these sacred truths to the ancient *rishis* who composed songs, mantras and texts in Vedic Sanskrit to express these truths. These songs and texts were then passed on over generations, from teacher to student, by chanting them aloud.

Memorizing those huge texts

The voluminous *Veds* are said to have been passed on verbally from generation to generation by a phenomenal human chain of memory, for an unknowingly long time. The knowledge was in the form of chants in various metres (structure of the verse) or *chhands* (छंद), perhaps to aid memory. Rhyme is not used in the Rig Ved and metres are regulated by the number of syllables in the verses – with about 100 styles of metres in use. The *chhands* of the mantra also acted as an error-correcting mechanism - any aberration in the *chhands* because of error in text or *swar* could be easily identified and corrected.

Eleven ways of reciting the Veds were designed to allow the complete and perfect memorization of the text and its pronunciation, including the Vedic pitch accent. Different disciples and their followers used these different styles, and when they were ultimately collated it is said that hardly any differences were found. In 2003, UNESCO proclaimed the tradition of Vedic chant a Masterpiece of the Oral and Intangible Heritage of Humanity.

The ways of recitation / memorization are *Sanhita* (संहिता), *Pad* (पद), *Kram* (क्रम), *Jata* (जटा), *Mala* (माला), *Shikha* (शिखा), *Rekha* (रेखा), *Dhwaj* (ध्वज), *Dand* (दंड), *Rath* (रथ) and *Ghan* (घन). The students were first taught to memorize the Veds using the simpler methods like continuous recitation (*sanhita path* - पाठ), word-by-word recitation (*pad path*) in which compounds (*sandhi*) are dissolved, and reciting the words in patterns (word1 word2, word2 word3, word3 word4...) (*kram path)*, before teaching them the other eight complex recitation styles. Does this not appear similar to the way our *sargam* is taught even today?

The *sanhita, pad* and *kram paths* can be described as the natural recitation styles or *prakritipath*. The remaining eight modes of chanting are classified as complex recitation styles or *vikritipath* as they involve reversing of the word order. Apparently, in the Vedic language, the backward chanting of words / changing their order does not alter the meanings.

The Veds

Eventually, the great *rishi*, Ved Vyas, collated and compiled all of the hymns and texts and split or classified these into four Veds. Each of the four Veds comprises of:

1. *Sanhitas*: One each per Ved, of the basic text of hymns and chants.
2. *Brahmans*: Directions for performance of rituals.
3. *Aranyaks*: For and by those living in forests
4. *Upanishads*: Texts revealing the ultimate spiritual truths and various ways to realize them.

The manuscript material (birch bark or palm leaves), had a short life of a few centuries only, as a result many of the early texts were lost over time. The present knowledge that we have has continued through various schools or *shakhas.* The Benares Sanskrit University reportedly has a Rig Ved manuscript of the mid-14th century though there are a number of older Ved manuscripts in Nepal that are dated from the 11th century CE onwards. Thus, as mentioned earlier, the compositions are from, say, 4000 BCE but the earliest words that are available in written form are several thousand years later.

The Collections of the Veds

The four **Sanhitas** (संहिता), or collections, of the four Veds comprise basically of hymns, except for the Yajur Ved which also has a lot of prose. These are a body of lyrical poetry distinguished by sophistication and beauty of thought as well as skill in the handling of language and metre. Ved Vyas taught the Rig Ved to his disciple Paila, the Yajur Ved to Vaishampayan, the Sam Ved to Jaimini, and the Atharva Ved to Sumantu.

The *Sanhita* of each Ved is the *Mantra* portion, and is a collection of hymns and mantras, some in prose. These were to be used in Vedic *yagyas* (यज्ञ) - a ritual through which man related with the gods / higher powers. In these Vedic ceremonies of worship / fire sacrifices or *yagyas*, offerings were made during the *puja* to please the Gods which could include fruits, vegetables, grain, animals (the latter are less common now).

Each of the four Ved *Sanhitas*, has one or more *Brahmans*, *Aranyaks*, and *Upanishads* associated with them —these are commentaries and elaborations on the *Sanhita* or the primary Vedic text, many in prose form. There are also varying versions on the chronological order – while one view is that they were simultaneous creations, it is more frequently said that the texts followed one another.

Besides the Veds are the **Vedangs** (वेदांग), or limbs of the

Veds, which expound the sciences required to understand and apply the Veds. The Vedangs relate to six fields and each of the fields had its own set(s) of books, as detailed further on. What followed much later than the *Shrutis* are the **Smriti** texts – those that were remembered—and these are huge in number. The **Up-veds** ("applied knowledge") are usually considered *Smriti* texts and deal with four traditional arts and sciences.

The Sanhitas of the Veds

The Rig Ved

The first and oldest collection is the **Rig Ved** (ऋग्वेद) which is a collection of *sukts* (सूक्त) or prayers in a poetic form, not in rhymes but in *chhands* / metres, with each style having its rules of the number of syllables etc. The *sukts* are songs and praises of various gods and contain much of the mythology and the most ancient Vedic ritual practices. Each *sukt* or poem or hymn contains verses or *mantras* (मंत्र) or *richas* (ऋचा) or *Riks* (ऋक्) — this latter word means *stuti, puja* or praise.

The Rig Ved is reportedly the oldest book in Sanskrit or any Indo-European language and shows the social, religious, political and economic background of the Rig-Vedic civilization. The words of the Veds do not reveal knowledge directly in their literal meaning, there are implied meanings and symbolism, the need for a guru to explain these is therefore considered essential.

The *Sanhita* of the Rig Ved contains *sukts* alone—1017 *sukts* with 10552 verses or *Riks*. To get an idea of the impressiveness of these texts, the download of the *Sanhita* of the Rig Ved alone runs into over 600 A4 size print pages. And it may be remembered all of this (along with the other texts of the *Veds*) had been memorized and passed down faithfully over generations, for thousands of years.

Rig Ved is built around a science of sound which comprehends the meaning and power of each letter, with pitch (*udatt* उदात्त – raised, *anudatt* अनुदात्त – low, and *svarit* स्वरित – high falling) indicated by means of horizontal and vertical lines below or above the alphabet. The hymns of the Rig Ved are neither the production of a single hand nor do they probably belong to any single age. Many of the hymns / *mantras* commonly recited today are from the Rig Ved.

The *sukts* are strongly religious in character; concerned with the worship of gods that are largely personifications of the powers of Nature. There are others that are narrative, philosophical, or even speculative. Most of the *sukts* in the Rig Ved are dedicated to specific deities, the most prominent are *Indra*, the leader of the *devtas* and the god of heaven and rain; *Agni,* the sacrificial fire and messenger of the gods; and *Som,* the ritual drink dedicated to Indra.

Others are the *Maruts* (storm gods and attendants of Indra); the *Ashvin kumars* (twin horsemen symbolizing sunrise and sunset, as also the doctors of the gods and the *devs* of ayurvedic medicine); *Mitra* (the friend) and *Varun* (one who encompasses and binds, the deliverer from evil). Sun is personified as *Surya*, but there are other solar deities too. Other natural phenomena include *Vayu* (the wind), *Dyaus* and *Prithvi* (Heaven and Earth) and their daughter *Ushas* (the dawn).

Rivers are deified as goddesses, most prominently the *Sapta*

Sindhu (seven rivers) and the *Saraswati* River. *Yam* is the first ancestor, the god of the underworld and death. *Rudra* (an early form of Shiv) is also mentioned. Amongst the prominent deities of today, "Vishnu of the three strides" is mentioned, but one does not find the others. The *sukts* are mainly invocations of these gods; they frequently refer to the genealogy of the gods and their past deeds of wonder.

As mentioned earlier, there are implied meanings and symbolism in our texts. Thus it has been said that *Agni* is not only fire as one would normally think, nor "the god of fire". He is that which is possessed of the quality of heat and color in all orders of life. He is the physical fire as well as the fire of knowledge and the colors in all objects one can see, the power of seeing, etc.

A great degree of skill and art is found in the composition of the *sukts* by the *rishis*, perhaps to make their prayers more acceptable to the gods. This has been compared to a vehicle put together by a deft craftsman, to fair and well-woven garments; or to a bride adorned for her lover, the gods being lauded and utterances given to emotions in the hearts of the *rishis*. It has been held that in some hymns there is also simple child-like astonishment on the phenomena of Nature – why does the sun not fall from the sky, where do the stars go at night, the waters of rivers constantly go to the ocean yet never fill it. An idea of the beauty of the Rig Ved may be had from the *Nasidiya Sukt* given at the end of this book.

The verses in the Rig Ved are more frequently arranged in accordance with the gods they praise - thus first we get the *sukts* addressed to Agni, then those to Indra etc. An older method of division is mechanical with the Rig Ved apportioned into 'eighths' or *Ashtaks* (अष्टक) of about equal length (and further subdivided into eight *Adhyays* (अध्याय) or 'lessons', and further into *Vargs* (वर्ग) or groups.

Another method of division of the Rig Ved is into 10 Mandals (मण्डल) or groups / books of *sukts*. Knowledge received from Parashar (the father of Ved Vyas), but composed by various rishis, is placed in the first Mandal. Six of the Mandals (II to VII), are each ascribed to a single family of rishis. Most of Mandal 3, including the **Gayatri Mantra** is credited to Vishwamitra, the fifth Mandal to Atri, and the sixth to the family of Angira. Mandal 7 (which also has the famous **Mritunjay Mantra**) is credited to Vashishth (वशिष्ठ). All the hymns In Mandal IX are addressed to the same deity, *Som*, with its groups based on metre not on authorship. The 10th Mandal is considered a later addition and has speculative hymns on the nature of creation. The Nasadiya Sukt is also part of this Mandal and is exceptionally remembered.

The Rig Ved is said to be the father of the other Veds. It was followed by Yajur and Sam Veds (Atharva Ved has a different style). Attention here shifts from praise and invocation of the Gods, to practice and rituals—the priest becomes the focus.

The Yajur Ved

The **Yajur Ved** (यजुर्वेद) is a liturgical (religious) collection of ceremonies and associated practices considered essential for following the religion. This was the main Ved used by the priests in ancient India and practically served as a guidebook of the mantras for the priest to chant. It contains *riks,* prose mantras and verses (called *Yajus*) used in ritual. It also deals with rites, their performance and the fruits of such rituals of worship. Besides some verses extracted from the Rig Ved, the Yajur Ved contains many original prose commentaries, the contents arranged in the order in which the verses were actually employed in the various rituals.

It has two branches called pure or white Yajur Ved, and mixed or black Yajur Ved (the **Shukla** and **Krishna Yajur Veds**). There is an interesting story on these two branches. It is said that rishi Vaishampayan, who had received the knowledge of the Yajur Ved from Ved Vyas, had a number of disciples. But due to a dispute he required one of his disciples, Yagyavalkya (याज्ञवल्क्य), to give back all the knowledge acquired. Yagyavalkya, in search of a non-human *guru*, prayed to the Sun and acquired the pure knowledge known as the Shukla Yajur Ved. The knowledge returned by Yagyavalkya was absorbed by the other disciples and became the Krishna Yajur Ved.

The Shukla Yajur Ved has only mantras in the form of *chhands* - it has 1975 mantras in 40 chapters, while the

Krishna Yajur Ved has seven *kands* (कांड) with 44 chapters of both *chhand* mantras and prose mantras besides a large number of prose prayers and procedures.

It is interesting to see that both the Shukla and the Krishna Yajur Veds also refer to numbers. While expressions of smaller numbers are seen even in the Rig Ved (e.g. nine-and-ninety, sixty thousand, a hundred thousand), here we see progressive numbers such as odd, even, multiples of fives etc. as also names of numbers in powers of ten going up to exceedingly large numbers (10 to the power of 17). Incidentally India brought the decimal system to the world, and our advanced thinking on numbers is visible here.

The Yajur Ved is the Ved of ritual, but on a deeper level, it sets forth a yogic practice for purifying the mind and awakening inner consciousness. The purpose is to unite the individual with the universal, the rituals of worship /sacrifices culminating in *Atmayagya* or Self-sacrifice − offering one's ego to the Divine.

The Sam Ved

The **Sam Ved** (सामवेद) *Sanhita* is purely a liturgical collection of melodies and has chants for the priest to sing at the *yagya*. Unlike the Yajur Ved, it does not have prose mantras and consists almost exclusively of mantras from the Rig Ved, mainly of the VIIth and IXth Mandal put to a different and more musical chant. These were meant to be sung to certain fixed melodies and are arranged in the order that was used for singing at *yagyas* and other auspicious occasions. A *Sam* (साम) is a mantra with a metre, which has to be sung according to the symbols indicated in the mantra.

The Sam Ved is the smallest of the Veds, yet its importance is high as it contains selected pieces of the Rig Ved and some from the other two Veds. It contains songs of praise of various gods such as *Agni*, *Surya* and *Som*. (*Som* has varied meanings - it is a plant, a drink made from the plant, a deity—the god of inspiration, full moon—the time to collect and drink, the cup that holds the drink, the Moon etc.).

A reduced version of the Rig Ved, the Sam Ved has 1875 mantras. Its secret is in its musical annotation and rendering. The order of the verses have been re-arranged, without reference to the order in the Rig Ved, but in accordance with the rituals in which they were to be used.

The *Sanhita* of the Sam Ved gives us only the texts as they are spoken. The melodies themselves were taught in the earliest days by oral repetition or by playing them on instruments. From a later date we have the so-called *Gaan* (गान) or 'song-books', which describe the melodies by notes, and in which the texts are recorded with all syllable-expansions, repetitions and insertions of syllables / complete words, various modulations, rests etc. The note marking here is by means of the figures 1, 2, 3 etc. or a few letters - written above the syllables.

Our (classical) music is said to have originated from the Sam Ved and our *sargam* to have evolved from its chants, which in turn were based on the three basic *swars*/pitch of the Rig Ved.

Usage of sukts by various priests

Various priests conducted the *hom* (होम) or *havan* using the *sukts* and mantras of the Veds. The Veds talk of different types of priests - the *Brahman* (ब्राह्मण) priest, the *Hotri* (होतृ) priest, the *Udgatri* (उद्गातृ) priest and the *Adhvaryu* (अध्वर्यु) priest. The *Brahman* (ब्राह्मण) priest played an important role and maintained continuity, integrity and purity of the rituals. He was helped by others. The *Hotri* (होतृ) priest chanted hymns from the Rig Ved and initiated the rituals by inviting the gods, the *Udgatri* (उद्गातृ) priest sang melodious hymns of praise and invocations from the Sam Ved and kept the ritual place ready for the descent of the gods, while the *Adhvaryu* (अध्वर्यु) priest who was responsible for the performance of the ritual proper, chanted hymns from the Yajur Ved and ensured that the offerings were correctly made to the gods.

During Vedic civilisation, material offerings were made to the gods after the conclusion of the songs and mantras praising the deities. The offerings presented to the gods consisted chiefly of *ghee*, curd, and fermented *som* juice, which was generally mixed with water or milk. All was thrown into the fire, which bore them, or their essences, to the gods. Fire has the capacity to consume anything - *Agni*, the fire god, thus became predominant in this form of worship. Till today, the practice of conducting *havans* continues, and these are performed at the end of a *puja*.

The Atharva Ved

The Atharva Ved (अथर्ववेद) is the last of the Veds and, with regard to history and sociology, is next in importance to the Rig Ved. It probably attained its present form considerably later than the Rig Ved from which it is significantly different, the two being complementary to each other in content. While some hymns of the Atharva Ved are considered to be even earlier than the earliest in the Rig Ved, it is said that the Atharva Ved continued to grow till after some of the Smriti texts. Some thoughts of the Atharva Ved are also found in the Xth Mandal of the Rig Ved.

Unlike the other three Veds, the hymns of Atharva Ved are of a more diverse character and are also simpler in language. The contents and focus of Atharva Ved is extremely varied. It contains topics dealing with philosophical questions inquiring about the nature of the universe like those in Rig Ved and yet it also contains topics dealing with magic and incantations used against opponents during rivalries, warfare etc.

Reportedly the oldest text dealing with medicine, the Atharva Ved also comprises prayers against enemies, sorcerers, fever, diseases and for atonement of mistakes made during the sacrificial ritual, as well as chants dealing with household and royal rites. It deals with medicine, military arts, magic, crafts etc. Thus it has charms to cure diseases, paralysis, leprosy, poison, imprecations against demons, sorcerers, and enemies, prayers for protection through talismans etc., rites for prolonging life and for fulfilling one's desires, building construction, trade and commerce, statecraft and penances. Some scholars do not accept this as a Ved and tend to speak only of three Veds.

The Atharva Ved does contain many *sukts* from the Rig Ved but also has some more popular magic spells which are outside the strictly ritual-knowledge orientation of the other Veds. It has 5987 mantras in 20 kands (कांड). According to tradition, the Atharva Ved was mainly composed by two groups of rishis known as the Atharvas and the Angiras, and its oldest name is Atharvangiras. It is also attributed to Bhrigu and Angira, with parts ascribed to Kaushik, Vashishth and Kashyap.

Veds - Beyond the Sanhitas

It is said that the creative period of the *Sanhitas* (more commonly referred to simply as the Veds) came to an end and was followed by a long period when there no longer seemed to be any need to offer new prayers to the gods but more meritorious to repeat those made by the *rishis* of bygone times and handed down over generations. The old hymns were thus gathered and acquired an ever-increasing sanctity. Creative energies were transferred to the elaboration of rituals with the importance of the hymns being in their applications to the ceremonies.

The Brahmans

The *Sanhita* of each Ved was followed by the **Brahmans** (ब्राह्मण) or Manuals of Rituals. The existing *Brahmans* are considered several centuries later than the *Sanhitas*; the oldest about 800 or 700 BCE. With the lapse of significant time after the Ved *Sanhitas*, language had also changed. The Brahmans are written entirely in prose, with the style sometimes missing the beauty of the *Sanhitas*. They attempt to explain the mutual relation of the sacred texts with the ceremonies, and also contain tales of the various incarnations or *avtars*.

Each of the *Brahmans* is associated with one of the *Sanhitas* or its recensions. The *Brahmans* may either form separate texts or can be partly integrated into the text of the *Sanhitas* as in the case of the Krishna Yajur Ved. They may also include the *Aranyaks* and Upanishads. A total of 19 *Brahmans* are extant in their entirety: two associated with the Rig Ved, six with the Yajur Ved, ten with the Sam Ved and one with the Atharva Ved. Chief among the *Brahmans* are the Aitreya and the Saptpath.

While the *Sanhitas* or the mantra portion used in the *yagyas* or rituals of worship (frequently translated or referred to as sacrifices) comprised the prayers or songs to be chanted, the *Brahmans* contain the rules and regulations for the *yagyas*. These ritual text books were intended to guide the priest through the complicated details of the rites.

The *Brahmans* are amplifications of the *Sanhitas* - they contain prose commentaries explaining the meaning of the mantras and rituals for the householder who, as the worshiper, now only looked on and worshiped by proxy. The priest had risen greatly in importance as he alone knew the sacred verses and the sacred rites. The externals of religion became all in all, everything depended on due performance of the rites, perhaps overshadowing the gods themselves. It is said that the Hindu ritual gradually grew into a stupendous system, the most elaborate and complex seen in the world.

The Aranyaks

The **Aranyaks** (आरण्यक) "wilderness texts" or "forest treaties" are a further development of the *Brahmans* and relate to the study of God and religion. The *Aranyaks* are the third part of the Veds and are considered to have been composed by people who meditated in the woods as recluses.

The *Aranyaks* deal with Brahm knowledge and meditation intended for those people who had retired into the forests (*vanprasth ashram*), and were thus unable to perform elaborate rituals which required many articles and accessories not procurable in forests. The texts also contain discussions and interpretations of dangerous rituals (to be studied outside the settlement). It is frequently read in secondary literature. An important *Aranyak* is the Taittiriya.

The *Aranyaks* do not give us rules for the performance of rituals of worship or explanations of the ceremonies, but provide us with explanations and meanings of the sacrificial religion. These were perhaps intended to be communicated by the *rishi* to his disciples in the solitude of the forests.

The *Aranyak* age was a period during which free thinking tried gradually to shake off the shackles of ritualism which had fettered it for a long time. It was thus that the *Aranyaks* could pave the way for the Upanishads, revive the philosophic speculation in the *Sanhitas*, and develop them in a manner which made the Upanishads the source of all philosophy that arose in the world of Hindu thought.

The Upanishads

The **Upanishads** (उपनिषद) primarily discuss Hindu philosophy and deal with the *alaukik* (अलौकिक) or that which is incomprehensible to the ordinary sense organs and to reasoning based on findings. Upanishad means "be seated at the feet of the *guru* to receive the teaching." Many of the Upanishads contain accounts of various debates between contemporary *rishis* in a guru-disciple manner. While even the Upanishads are not read by the common man, amongst the Vedic books (*shrutis*) it is these, or their translations / commentaries, which are studied as religious texts. Several current Hindu beliefs are based on the Upanishads.

The principal Upanishads, of which there are traditionally ten to thirteen (with several later additions taking the number to 108 or 112 or even more), were probably composed between 800 and 100 BCE. The Upanishads are typically understood as an extension of the Veds; they are also collectively known as *Vedant* or the "completion" of the Veds. The oldest and longest of the Upanishads are the Brihad-Aranyak Upanishad and the Chhandogya Upanishad (circa 7th century BCE).

The Upanishads more clearly set out the Vedic / Hindu doctrines of self-realization, *yog* (योग,(meditation, *karm* (कर्म) and reincarnation. However, the Upanishads significantly reject many of the early Vedic ideas and practices e.g. the multiple deities of the *Sanhitas*, arguing that all one gets from such ritual is merely materialistic. The sages or *rishis* who composed the Upanishads sought something more—ultimate, eternal salvation. In general the Upanishads postulate a single, eternal, impersonal divine force that animates and permeates the entire cosmos—Brahm (ब्रह्म).

An important figure in the Upanishads is the sage Yagyavalkya (याज्ञवल्क्य). Most of the great teachings of later Hindu philosophy derive from him. He taught the doctrine of "**neti-neti**", the view that truth can be found only through the negation of all thoughts about it - "this is not the Truth, the Truth is still beyond – beyond our reach, beyond our description, and beyond our understanding." Or more simply, (God is) "Not this, not this"; God cannot be characterized by any quality including virtues, trait, character, size, shape, attribute, time etc.

In most cases, the concluding parts of the *Aranyaks* are the Upanishads. Some Veds have the entire series of *Sanhita, Brahman, Aranyak* and Upanishads, while in others the Upanishad may be attached to the *Sanhita* or the *Brahman* directly or may even be independent. Similarly there is also not necessarily only one *Brahman* attached to a *Sanhita*. Though the older Upanishads are usually affixed to a particular *Sanhita*, through a *Brahman* or *Aranyak*; the more recent ones are not.

The four parts of each Ved are also said to be linked to the four stages of a person's life. Thus the *Sanhitas* were studied by the student *brahamachari*, the householder followed the injunctions of the *Brahmans*, the forest dweller practiced contemplation according to the *Aranyaks* and the renouncer or *sanyasi* was guided by the wisdom of the Upanishads[1].

Veds deal with both action and knowledge. Thus in these texts there is *karmkand* (ritualistic action, sacrifice / *yagyas* etc. for the attainment of material prosperity on earth, and joy in heaven after death) and also *gyankand* (knowledge through which one is liberated from ignorance and enabled to realize the highest good). The *Sanhitas* and *Brahmans* deal with action or *Karmkand* as worship (*upasana*) for the attainment of some desired objects. The *Aranyaks* and the Upanishads deal with *gyankand* or meditations for the attainment of knowledge and merging with Brahm.

Each Upanishad is complete in itself, and the texts are primarily inspirational. The Upanishads do not provide easy answers, but rather lead the reader to become conscious of the questions, and to experience one's own spiritual being and connection to the universe. Creation, man's actions and reactions, and cause and effect are all part of the Upanishads. While each Upanishad is independent of the others, many themes, phrases, or even several verses are found repeated (in another Upanishad or the Bhagvad Gita or even in the same Upanishad). The lyrics of the Upanishads cannot be quickly skimmed. It is said that reading them again and again reveals rich, profound, and beautiful truths.

---

[1] See The Upanishads by Swami Nikhilananda

Inter-linkages of the texts of Upanishads are also observed. The Aitareya Aranyak, which is a part of the Aiterya Brahman, has philosophical speculations under the names of *pran* and *purush* (its concluding part is the Aitareya Upanishad). Some thoughts or even complete verses of Aitareya Aranyak are found repeated in the Kaushitaki Upanishad, which is part of the Kaushitaki Brahman (which also has parts of the Aitreya Aranyak) through the Kaushitaki Aranyak.

A little more on ten of the major Upanishads is given further on in this book.

Other associated texts

The **Anukramanis** (अनुक्रमणी) are systematic indices of Vedic hymns. The *rishi* Shaunak (and others) compiled the *Anukramanis*, which document the sage who heard each verse from the gods, the deity that each verse is addressed to, and the *Chhand* or metre of each hymn.

There are two other important groups of supplementary literature considered *Smriti* texts, but related closely to the Veds themselves, and timed more or less simultaneously with the production of the principal Upanishads.

The Vedangs

A.   The **Vedangs** (वेदांग), or literally limbs of the Veds, are expositions on the sciences required to understand and apply the Veds. It is said that as people gradually abandoned their semi-nomadic lifestyle and began to settle permanently, the rituals became increasingly complex, giving rise to developments in mathematics, geometry, grammar and astrology. The six Vedangs relate to six fields, and each field had its own set(s) of books. Traditionally, only *Vyakaran* and *Nirukt* are common to the four Veds, while the others are particular to the individual Ved. The Vedangs are:

(1) **Shiksha** (शिक्षा) texts and **Pratishakhyas.** The Shiksha texts are on *varnmala, swar* and *varn* etc. The **Pratishakhyas** (प्रतिशाख्य) are phonetic treatises frequently associated with an individual Ved or even a specific recension. These texts explain the proper articulation, pronunciation, intonation and the *sandhi* rules (rules of connecting / joining words) of the Vedic texts.

(2) **Chhands** (छंद) (metre). The verses of the Veds have a variety of different metres, grouped by the number of lines in a verse, and by the number of syllables in a line. The methodical rhythmic recitation was mandatory to keep the purity of text, and the study of Vedic metre is one of the six Vedang disciplines. The most important text on *chhands* is the Chhand Shastra, ascribed to Pingal (पिङ्गल) circa 2nd century BCE.

(3) **Vyakaran** (व्याकरण). This deals with the study of Sanskrit grammar, usage of words and sentences, root words and complex sentence structures. This can be said to be represented by Panini's (पाणिनि) grammar known as

Ashtadhyayi (अष्टाध्यायी). (c. 6th to 4th century BCE).

(4) **Nirukt** (निरुक्त) or lexicon. This discusses and defines difficult / Vedic words, and is represented by the Nirukt of Yask (यास्क) (c. 6th century BCE).

(5) **Jyotish** (ज्योतिष). A system of astronomy and astrology used to determine the right times for rituals, and includes mathematics and *vastu-shastra*. The Vedang Jyotish (वेदाङ्ग ज्योतिष) is one of earliest known texts on astronomy and astrology composed by Lagadha (c. 400 BCE)

(6) **Kalpa** (कल्प) sutras are texts on rituals. Here the *Shraut* (श्रौत) texts cover the due performance of rituals. The *Dharm sutras* (also discussed further on in this book) are on how to live life according to *dharm*. There are also the *Grihya sutras* (गृह्यसूत्र) on how to perform domestic rites, and *Shulba sutras* (शुल्बसूत्र) on construction of the *yagya sthal* / ceremonial fireplace etc. The *Shulba sutras* are known for mathematics, geometry etc.

Incidentally the ancient books mentioned above are amongst the most significant / well-known. They in turn sometimes refer to much older texts of several centuries earlier which might not be available.

The Up-Veds

B. The **Up-veds** (उपवेद) ("applied knowledge") supplement the

Veds with more specific applications of Vedic teachings. They are usually considered *Smriti* texts and deal with the four traditional arts and sciences. The list of subjects included in this class differs among sources.

1. **Ayur-ved** (आयुर्वेद) (medicine), deals with the science of life and the body. It is considered to be a system of natural and holistic medicine.

2. **Gandharva-ved** (गन्धर्ववेद) (music and dance), is the text for *sangeet* (music) comprising of singing, playing and dance.

3. **Dhanur-ved** (धनुर्वेद) (warfare, archery). While *dhanur* means bow, this subject deals not only with archery, but the entire science of warfare. It includes information on battle plans and formations, preparation and training of different arms of the military, etc.

4. **Arth-shastra** (अर्थ शास्त्र) (public administration, governance, economy) deals with the science of statecraft. It provides details on rulership, different areas of government and society.

Some however hold the fourth Up-ved (उपवेद) to be **Sthapatya-ved** (स्थापत्यवेद) (engineering and architecture).

Background to the Smriti Texts

The next set of our Scriptures are the **Smritis** (स्मृति). *Smriti* literature refers to 'memorized' or 'remembered' poetry and epics. While *Shrutis* are authorless works or *apaurushey granths* (अपौरुषेय ग्रन्थ), *Smritis* are the words of our rishis — they are considered to be of human, not divine, origin. Or to put it simply, the *Smriti* manuscripts have known authors. All authoritative writings outside the Veds are collectively referred to as *Smritis*.

These are generally later texts and help explain the *Shruti* scriptures. The language being less cryptic, they are more easily understood and hence more popular. They use symbolism and mythology to clarify and contain some of the most beautiful and exciting stories. In terms of number and volume, if the *Shruti* texts are large, the *Smritis* can be considered overwhelming.

The period, beginning from around 500 BCE saw the composition of further writings such as the *Dharm Sutras* and *Shastras*, the two Epics (the Mahabharat and the Ramayan), and subsequently the *Purans* that contain many of the stories still popular today.

During this period, the importance of the Vedic fire sacrifice or *yagya* reduced with the development of devotional worship (*puja*) to images of deities in temples.

Smriti scriptures include five distinct groups of writings (not in chronological order):

- *Itihas* (History or Epics)

- *Agams* - Sectarian Scriptures arising out of differences amongst different religious groups.

- *Purans* - Mythology

- *Darshans* - Manuals of Philosophy

- *Dharm Shastras* - Law Codes

Itihas

Amongst the *Itihas* (histories), we have two great epics, the Ramayan (रामायण) and the Mahabharat (महाभारत). Both the epics were written after the beginning of the 6th century BCE, with changes being made till the 2nd century CE. The events they narrate are said to have happened much before the actual writing.

Ramayan

The **Ramayan** is the most popular of our epics, composed in Sanskrit by Valmiki (the erstwhile *daku* Ratnakar) around 4th or 2nd centuries BCE with later additions up to the 3rd century CE. It has 24,000 verses in seven books or *kands* (though some hold that the first and the last books were not composed by him). The verses in the Ramayan are written in a 32-syllable metre called *anustubh*.

The happenings narrated in the epic are based in the *Treta Yug* (the second of four *yugs* in the perennial cycles of *yugs*). Shri Ramchandra or Ram, the eldest son of King Dashrath, of the Sun Dynasty or *Ikshvaku* (इक्ष्वाकु) dynasty is the seventh incarnation of Vishnu – he is said to have come into prominence with this epic.

Shri Ramchandra killed the *rakshas* (राक्षस) king Ravan of Lanka who had become the all-powerful ruler of the three worlds, earth, heaven and the netherworld (*patal* पाताल). Thereafter Shri Ram is said to have ruled the Kingdom of

Kosal (कोसल) from Ayodhya, for a golden age known as the *ramrajya*. Many legends are inter-woven in this epic.

It presents the teachings of the Veds and the ancient Hindu sages in a narrative tale, interspersed with philosophical and devotional facets. Ramayan brings to the fore the Hindu concept of rebirth, with the tale frequently referring to the actions of persons, *rishis* and even the gods in their previous lives. These form the basis for their presence during the events in this saga, and several of these also find mention in various Purans.

The text survives in several partial and complete manuscripts, the oldest of which is reportedly a palm-leaf manuscript found in Nepal and dated to the 11th century CE.

The Ramayan has been retold by other writers at different times in different languages (Tamil, Telugu, and Assamese etc. besides in several countries abroad). Its rendition in Awadhi — a dialect of Hindi spoken in eastern parts of Uttar Pradesh and in Bihar - by Tulsidas (c. 16th century CE) is known as "**Ramcharitmanas**" and has several differences vis-à-vis Valmiki's Ramayan.

Gods of today — the Trinity, Hanuman, Ganesh, Parvati to name a few are present in this epic. *Sundar Kand* (सुंदरकाण्ड), the fifth book of the Ramayan depicts the adventures of Hanuman and its recitation is a significant religious practice.

Incidentally about 50 years back, in Vadodra, several scholars examined more than 2,000 palm leaf and other manuscripts in various scripts and undertook the monumental task of compiling the 'Critical Edition of Valmiki's Ramayana' to arrive at the closest resemblance to Valmiki's original text.

Mahabharat

Included in the *Itihas* is the **Mahabharat.** Though the origins of this epic probably fall between the 8th and 9th centuries BCE, the oldest preserved parts of the text are thought to be not much older than 4th century BCE, with the text probably reaching its final form by c. 4th century CE.

It contains 110,000 couplets (in 18 sections called *parvs*) reportedly making it the longest poem and greatest epic in world literature. With about 1.8 million words in total, the Mahabharat is roughly ten times the length of the Iliad and the Odyssey combined, and about four times the length of the Ramayan. The tale is said to have been extended from a shorter version of 24,000 verses simply called Bharat.

The Mahabharat is based in the *Dvapar Yug* (the third *yug*) and this too adopts the story within a story style, the primary story being recited by the *rishi* Vaishampayan, a disciple of Vyas, to King Janamejay (जनमेजय), the great-grandson of the Pandav prince Arjun. This epic narrates the story of the Kauravs and the Pandavs for the kingship of Hastinapur, and the historical eighteen day battle at Kurukshetra, near Delhi. While the story has been penned down by Shri Ganesh, Ved Vyas is the author and also a character in the Mahabharat.

Here Vishnu's incarnation as Krishna, is as the cousin of the Pandavs and, during the war, he is the charioteer and mentor of Arjun (the third Pandav brother). The book is a treasure house of Indian wisdom and tradition. It holds within it a code of life and guidance for ethical, social and spiritual relations. It deals with topics that include the creation of the world, history of the sages, *dharm*, politics, military strategies, proper behavior of a king, and ways of spirituality and devotion to God.

The epic includes the essence of the Upanishads and other Vedic teachings, and the famous Bhagvad Gita, as also discourses by Bhishma and learned sages to Yuddhishtra on the duties of a ruler, the rule of law, instructions on *dharm* for those close to the leader etc. It also has the *Anugita*, Krishna's second discourse to Arjun, this time well after the war is over, Yuddhishtra is king and Krishna is departing for Dwarka. It contains information about the nature of Brahm, but is not considered as lucid or as beautiful as the Bhagvad Gita, nor is it as well known and discussed.

Bhagvad Gita

The **Bhagvad Gita** (भगवद गीता) or the **Srimadbhagvadgita** (श्रीमद्भगवद्गीता) is a 700–verse Hindu scripture from chapters 25 to 42 of the Bhishma-*parv* (the 6th) of the Mahabharat. It is estimated to have been written about the 5th to 2nd century BCE. This scripture contains a conversation between Arjun and his guide Krishna (the eighth incarnation of Vishnu) on a variety of philosophical issues. Arjun, the courageous warrior, finds it difficult to fight against his own elders, uncles and cousins. Krishna teaches that it is Arjun's duty as a Kshatriya warrior to fight against *adharm*, explaining the importance of *dharm* over *adharm*. On Arjun's request, he reveals His true form and teaches about bhakti or devotion, Brahm etc.

The Bhagvad Gita is the direct instruction from God to his devotee and contains knowledge of the soul, law of *karm*, reincarnation, knowledge of and on attaining the Supreme (Brahm), and the essential purpose of life. Though a part of the Mahabharat and hence a *Smriti*, it is philosophical in nature and its authority and influence is such that it is usually raised to the status of an Upanishad.

Sankhya yog or the path of knowledge as the means of liberation has been described in Chapter 2 and is considered an important chapter. It teaches that whereas the body is transitory, the Self within is eternal and indestructible. Just as a man casts off his worn-out clothes and puts on new ones, so also the Self casts off it's worn out body and enters another that is new. Death and birth are certain and every being passes through the repeated cycles of death and birth. The wise therefore do not grieve for those who are dead or for those who are living. All living creatures existed before their birth, they exist now and would exist in future too.

The Gita explains that just as a man experiences his existence before sleep, during sleep and after sleep, this existence too is continuous even though the body is ever-changing and ultimately perishes one day to acquire another. We too shall not cease to exist even after the disappearance of our present bodies. While the biological body is bound by time and space, the Self's existence is independent of time and space.

The Bhagvad Gita uses the term "*yog*" (योग) extensively in a variety of ways and introduces three prominent types of yog:

- *Gyan yog*: The yog of knowledge.
- *Karm yog*: The yog of action.
- *Bhakti yog*: The yog of devotion or of supreme faith.

Each of these three *yogs* set out different paths. *Sankhya yog* or *gyan yog* or the path of knowledge, which directly reveals the true nature of the Self, is meant for very rare seekers. The follower of *Karm Yog* engages in action without any desire for, or attachment to, the result of such action. He is engaged in performance of his duty, regards himself as an instrument of God, and is protected from the cycle of birth and death. A well-known saying is Krishna's teaching: "*Karmany evadhikaraste Ma Phaleshu Kadachan*" (कर्मण्येवाधिकारस्ते मा फलेषु कदाचन) or "You have the right to perform your actions, but you are not entitled to the fruits of the actions". *Bhakti-yog*, or the path of devotion, is revealed as the best and simplest means for regaining awareness of our relationship with the Supreme Being. Here one surrenders to God in totality with full love, faith and trust.

Agams and Tantras

The *Agams* (आगम) are sectarian scriptures dealing with the worship of a particular aspect of God and prescribing detailed courses of discipline for the worshipper. Few of the *Agams* have been published (or even collected) and knowledge of these is yet to fully emerge. The origin and chronology of Agamic religions remain uncertain. The *Agams* are also considered to be of divine origin, perhaps pre-Vedic, and passed on in a *guru-shishya* tradition. The written texts in Sanskrit / Tamil (actually Granthi — the old Tamil script) are said to be circa 10th century CE. Followers consider them as authoritative and as sacred as the Veds (the latter are also called *Nigams*), and as philosophical as the Upanishads. References to Agamic traditions are said to be found in the Atharva Ved.

The term *Agam* primarily means tradition. It also helps to understand things correctly and comprehensively. The *Agams* deal with *Mantra, Yantra* and *Tantra* (i.e. forms/representatives of God — sound, symbolic diagrams, and procedures or rituals). The most widespread rituals of worship today are *Agamic*. The *Agam* methods are worship of images of God through rituals (*Tantra*), symbolic charts (*Yantra*) and verbal symbols (*Mantra*). The *Agams* regard devotion and complete submission to the deity as fundamental to the pursuit of its aim, and hopes that eventually, by the grace of the worshipped deity, wisdom and enlightenment would follow.

Mantras are sacred utterances, sounds, or a syllable, word etc. With the repetition of mantras, attention gets directed to the source of the sound and the mind gets engaged.

Yantras are geometric designs acting as tools assisting in contemplation, concentration and meditation. The *Yantra* provides a focal point and when the mind is concentrated on a single, simple object, mental chatter ceases. *Yantras* are usually designed so that the eye is carried into the center, and very often they are symmetrical.

The word *Tantra* is made from the joining of *tanoti* (expansion) & *trayati* (liberation), which means liberation of energy and expansion of consciousness, and its principles form the basis of all yogic practices. *Tantra* rituals are individualistic in character and are in the nature of direct communication between the worshipper and his or her personal deity. A *Tantra* ritual is carried out in quiet privacy.

Temple worship is a combination of dissimilar modes of worship. At the temple, both the *Agamic* worship and the *Tantric* rituals take place. Several *Agamic* rites are conducted in the presence of the devotees while *Tantric* rituals are conducted by the priests in the privacy of the sanctum away from public gaze and are accompanied by the chanting of passages and mantras taken from Veds.

Agams are scriptures chiefly constituting the methods of temple construction and creation of idols, worship of deities, philosophical doctrines, meditative practices, four kinds of *yog* etc. *Agamic* traditions have been the sources of *Yog* and self-realization concepts, including *Kundalini Yog*. The traditions of today's Hinduism are closer to the *Agams* than the Veds. *Agams* deal with four topics:

- *Charya* (चर्या or doing) - lays down rules for daily worship (*puja*), observances of religious rites, rituals, festivals and *prayaschits*.
- *Kriya* (क्रिया or action) - consists of rules for construction of temples, sculpting, carving, and consecration of idols of deities for worship in temples, different forms of initiations or *diksha*.
- *Yog* (योग or meditation) - concentrates on physical and mental disciplines.
- *Gyan* (ज्ञान or knowledge) - consists of philosophical and spiritual knowledge, knowledge of reality and liberation.

Agams are sometimes also called the fifth Ved and considered as part of *Shrutis* with the above four parts likened to the four parts of the Veds. Some popular *agam-*based religions are those of Shaiva (Shiv), Vaishnav (Vishnu), Shakt (Shakti), others are Ganapathy (Ganesh), Kaumara (Kartikeya or Skand), Soura (Surya), Bhairava (Bhairav) etc. There exist 28 Shaiva, 77 Shakt and 215 Vaishnav Agams, besides a large number of *up-agams*. Incidentally there are Buddhist and Jain *Agams* too.

The ritualistic pattern of worship in the *Agamic* religions differs from the Vedic form. The Vedic *yagyas* do not require idols and shrines and are collective in form where a number of priests, specialized in each discipline of the sacrificial aspects, participate. On the other hand, the *Agamic* religions are based on idols with *puja* as means of worship. The *Agams* state three essential requirements for a place of pilgrimage - *Sthal* refers to the temple, *Tīrth*, to the temple tank and *Murti* to the deity worshipped. Elaborate rules are laid out in the *Agams* for *Shilpa* (the art of sculpture) describing the quality requirements of the places where temples are to be built, the kind of images to be installed, the materials from which they are to be made, their dimensions, proportions, air circulation, lighting in the temple complex etc. The rituals followed in worship services each day at the temple also follow rules laid out in the *Agams*.

The *Agams* are considered to be divine revelations, or *Shruti*, imparted by Vishnu, or between Shiv and Parvati. Shiv created each *tantra* as a combination of his five universal energies, or *shaktis: chit shakti* (energy of all-consciousness), *anand shakti* (energy of all-bliss), *iccha shakti* (energy of all-will), *gyan shakti* (energy of all-knowledge), and *kriya shakti* (energy of all-action).

Purans

The *Purans* (पुराण) are a genre of important religious texts, notably consisting of narratives of the history of the universe from creation to destruction, genealogies of kings, heroes and sages, and descriptions of Hindu cosmology, philosophy, and geography. These ancient texts eulogize various deities, primarily the divine *Trimurti* – Brahma (ब्रह्मा), Vishnu (विष्णु) and Mahesh or Shiv (शिव). The Purans explain the creation and the dissolution of the universe, rules for living, descriptions of various worlds, and contain many popular myths and stories. Individual Purans usually give prominence to a particular deity, employing an abundance of religious and philosophical concepts.

The essence of the Purans is to introduce the feeling of *bhakti* and dedication towards a personal form of God. The Purans clarify that the grace of God is never at random nor the consequence of any amount of good actions or *yog* or austerity. It is automatically experienced when a soul lovingly and totally submits herself to God. This loving submission is *bhakti*. Good actions on the other hand result in a sojourn in heaven (of appropriate length), with a rebirth again, but not to *moksh* (मोक्ष), which is eternal salvation.

The Purans are usually written in the form of stories narrated by one person to another, with many such narratives interwoven. They are medieval collections of laws, stories, and philosophy that largely reflect the teachings of older scriptures and also illustrate them with beautiful tales and concrete examples. The presentation of this vast literature in the form of stories, parables and myths helps in understanding. The Purans, in general, are for all kinds of people, including an ordinary family person who is deeply attached to his or her family and friends.

There are many *Purans* but eighteen are considered to be Maha Purans, or Great Purans, Many deal with the same or similar matters. There are many gods in the Hindu beliefs, the primary are Brahma regarded as the creator, Vishnu as the preserver, and Shiv as the destroyer. Since all three are important gods, the texts glorify each but the relative emphasis often varies from text to text. The eighteen mahapurans are sometimes divided into three groups of six each, which glorify Vishnu, Brahma and Shiv.

All the Purans are said to be authored by Ved Vyas. Incidentally, Vyas is like a designation, and there is a Vyas seat (of discourse). There is said to be one Vyas in each *Dwapar Yug*, living perhaps till the next cycle. The present Vyas *is Krishna Dwapayan*. He is also known as Ved Vyas since he split the collection of mantras and collated them into the four sets that comprise the Veds. He is the one who was present as a character in the Mahabharat and also wrote it, besides writing all the Purans.

Two aspects of the Purans are particularly noteworthy. First, that there are a vast array of characters and these appear across the various Purans, along with their births and rebirths. Several generations and a very large number of events are covered. Despite this, all aspects (characters, relationships, background, events etc.) maintain their integrity across the various Purans and contradictions are not seen. Second, that the books are voluminous – the Srimad Bhagvat Mahapuran alone for example, with 18,000 verses, runs into approx. 1000 print pages.

The Brahma Purans

The six *purans*, prominently *rajsik* and dedicated to **Brahma,** the Creator, are the Brahma Puran (24,000 verses), Bhavishya Puran (14,500 verses), Brahma Vaivart Puran (18,000 verses), Brahmand Puran (12,000 verses), Markandeya Puran (9,000 verses - dialogue between *rishi* Markandeya and Jaimini, a disciple of Vyas), and Vaman Puran (10,000 verses). The Devi Mahatmya (देवीमाहात्म्य), also known as the Durga Saptashati (दुर्गासप्तशती) is a part of the Markandeya Puran and is considered an important text of Shaktism.

The Vishnu Purans

The six predominantly *satvik* (*sattvagun pradhan*) purans are dedicated to Vishnu.

The **Bhagvat Puran** (भागवतपुराण) or **Srimad Bhagvat Mahapuran** with 18,000 verses divided into twelve cantos (volumes) is authored by Ved Vyas and recited first by his son Shuk to the dying king Parikshit, the grandson of Arjun. It is one of the greatest purans, with its focus on *bhakti* to the

Supreme God Vishnu or Narayan, the Preserver. It includes many well-known stories including the various *avtars* of Vishnu. The tenth canto or *adhyaya* is the essence of Srimad Bhagvat and contains the stories of Shri Krishna, both as the cowherd boy of Vrindavan and later as the powerful king of Dwarka. The eleventh canto summarizes the philosophies of Hindu religion. *(Note: If only one book is to be read to get an overview of Hindu religion, it is perhaps this one).*

The Srimad Bhagvat places at different points of the vast timespan of the present *Kalp*, all the great and revered figures. The *Matsya avtar* comes in the dawn before the break of the present *Kalp*. The *Varah* and *Narsingh avtars* along with Dhruv, later immortalized as the Pole Star, come in the first *Manvantar* and the *Kurm avtar* in the sixth *Manvantar*. Ram, Krishna and Vyas come in the twenty-eighth *Mahayug* of the seventh *Manvantar* (our present *Manvantar*).

(Note: Our ancient scriptures have visualized a phenomenal time span. Thus the four yugs (Satya, Treta, Dwapar and Kali yugs) make one Mahayug, which is 43,20,000 years long. 71 Mahayugs are one Manvantar and 1000 Mahayugs are a Kalp. The later is one day —not night—in the life of Brahma the Creator. And this goes on!).

The **Garud Puran** (गरुड़ पुराण) also known as Suparn Puran with 19,000 verses has a dialog between Vishnu and Garud, the King of Birds in its first part. The latter half of the Garud

Puran deals with life after death, funeral rites, *karm* and its after effects, and is frequently recited as a part of funeral rites or *Antyesti* or *Antim Sanskar* / while cremating the dead.

The other purans dedicated to **Vishnu** are the Vishnu Puran (23,000 verses presented as a dialogue between Parashar and his disciple Maitreya, it also contains a prophecy about Kalki, a future *avtar*), Narad or Naradiya Puran (25,000 verses - dialogue between sage Narad and Sanatkumar), Padma Puran (55,000 verses) and Varah Puran (10,000 verses).

The Shiv Purans

The six purans that are *tamsik* and glorify Shiv are Shiv Puran (24,000 verses), Ling Puran (11,000 verses), Skand Puran (81,100 verses – the largest Mahapuran and recited by Sage Vyas; Skand or Kartikeya is the son of Shiv), Agni Puran (15,400 verses), Kurm Puran (17,000 verses) and Matsya Puran (14,000 verses - so named because it was first recited by Vishnu himself, in his incarnation of a fish).

Other Purans of note are the Vayu Puran (24,000 verses), the Kalki Puran and the Harivansh Puran (16,000 verses). The last is more often considered *itihas* and attached to the Mahabharat as it describes the further life of Krishna up to his departure from earth – this point being the start of the Kaliyug – the fourth and last in the cycle of yugs.

Other Purans

Besides these, are the **Up-purans** (उपपुराण) such as the Sanat-kumar, Narsingh, Brihan-naradiya, Shiv-rahasya, Durvasa, Kapil, Bhargava, Varun, Kalika, Samba, Nandi, Surya, Parashar, Vashishth, Devi-Bhagvat, Ganesh, Mudgal, and Hamsa. These are considered ancillary or secondary texts with no agreement on which they are or even on how many (some say eighteen, others hold these to be very many more). The extant Up-purans can be broadly divided into six groups according to the sectarian views found in these texts: Vaishnav, Shakta, Shaiva, Saura, Ganapathy and non-sectarian.

Then we have the **Sthal Purans** which are stories of places and deal with traditions about temples and shrines, and the **Kul Purans** which deal with the origins of various castes.

Darshans

Hindu philosophy is traditionally divided into six *astik* (आस्तिक) or orthodox schools of thought or *darshans* (दर्शन) - views that accept the Veds as supreme revealed scriptures, as against the unorthodox views of Buddhism / Jainism. The **Darshan Shastras,** defining six schools of Vedic Philosophy (*Shad-Darshan* षड दर्शन*)* in the form of Sutras or maxims, are considered to be Manuals of Philosophy. Each system has its *Sutrakar*, i.e. the one great *rishi* who systematized the doctrines of the school. They generally deal with four topics:

1. Existence and nature of Brahm (ब्रह्म) (the one Supreme God)
2. Nature of the *jiv* or the individual soul
3. Creation of the *jagat* or the world
4. *Moksh* or liberation, and the disciplines that lead to it.

Our philosophy goes into very precise detail about the nature of reality, the structure and function of the human psyche and how the relationship between the two have important implications for human salvation (*moksh* मोक्ष). *Rishis* centered philosophy on an assumption that there is a unitary underlying order (*rit* - ऋत) in the universe, which is all pervasive and omniscient. The efforts by various schools were concentrated on explaining this order and the entity at its source (Brahm). The concept of natural law (*Dharm* धर्म) provided a basis for understanding questions of how life on earth should be lived.

The six classical philosophies and their *darshan sutras* are:

Sankhya Philosophy

The **Sankhya philosophy** (सांख्य दर्शन) of Sage Kapil (कपिल) c. 6th century BCE is regarded as the oldest of the orthodox philosophical systems and is based on the Upanishads. According to Sankhya, the universe consists of two realities: *Purush* (consciousness) and *Prakriti* (Nature, matter)—the experiencer and the experienced, the passive enjoyer (*bhogta*) and the enjoyed (*bhogya*).

Prakriti has three basic attributes or modes – *Satva* (related to purity, brightness, happiness, poise, fineness, lightness, illumination, and joy), *Rajas* (related to dynamism, activity, motion, excitation, and pain) and *Tamas* (inertia, coarseness, heaviness, obstruction, sloth, ignorance, insensitivity and inaction).

Prakriti bifurcates into animate and inanimate, and consists of 24 elements (*tattvas*) – these are *Prakriti* (in its three modes or attributes), the three aspects of the *antahkaran* (अंतःकरण - ego, mind, intelligence), the five gross elements or *mahabhuts* (ether, air, fire, water, earth), the five sense objects or *tanmatras* (sound, touch, sight, taste, smell), the five knowledge-acquiring senses or *gyanendriyas* (ear, skin, eye, tongue, nose), and the five working senses or *karmendriyas* (voice, legs, arms, reproductive organs, evacuating organs).

Purush (the 25th element) separates out into countless *Jivs* or souls. *Jiv* is bound to *Prakriti* due to desire and the end of this bondage is *moksh*. The objective of Sankhya is discrimination obtained by knowledge of the knower (*purush*) and of Nature (*prakriti*) – both manifest (visible - *vyakt*) and unmanifest (invisible - *avyakt*) (व्यक्त and अव्यक्त, प्रकट and अप्रकट). Lack of this knowledge is the source of binding; gaining the right knowledge / differentiation of the two is the source of liberation or *moksh*. Incidentally Sankhya Philosophy recognizes spirit and matter, but not the supreme spirit.

Panchshikha, a contemporary of King Janak, is reported to have written 60,000 verses on the nature of Prakriti, Self etc. The earliest surviving authoritative text on classical Sankhya philosophy is Sankhya Karika (सांख्यकारिका) (c. 200–400 CE) of Ishvarkrishna.

Yog Philosophy

The **Yog philosophy** (योग दर्शन) of sage Patanjali (पतंजलि) puts into practice the theory of Sankhya Philosophy. Additionally, Yog also holds that there is one Supreme *Purush* (God) who is above all other *purush*. Self-training for understanding the unity of *Atma* and Brahm is called Yog. (Yog means addition or joining—with Brahm).

Here the consciousness is called *chitt* (चित्त) and comprises of intellect, ego and mind. *Chitt* is subject to five afflictions – ignorance (*avidya*), false identification of the Self with the body and the mind *(asmita)*, attachment *(rag)*, aversion *(dvesh)* and fear of death *(abhinivesh)*.

Patanjali in his Yog Sutras (c. 2nd century BCE or 4th CE) lays emphasis on complete control and mastery of *chitt*. He proposes the practice of certain physical and mental exercises, which form the basis of *Ashtang Yog* (अष्टांग योग).

The eight steps comprise *yam* (यम) or observances / absentations or moral code, *niyam* (नियम) or rules / restraints for self-discipline and spiritual study, *asan* (आसन) or body posture (for sitting in meditation and for making the body and mind more harmonious), *pranayam* (प्राणायाम) or breath control – breathing methods aimed at better control of life energies or *pran, Pratyahar* (प्रत्याहार) or withdrawal of senses—an inward-turning, *dharana* (धारणा) or concentration /contemplation or a focussing for a long time for essential basic awareness, *Dhyan* (ध्यान) or deep meditation and *Samadhi* (समाधि) or self-absorption—a higher level of meditation, to be had from sustained *dhyan*.

The *yams* or social ethics are *Ahinsa* (अहिंसा) or non-harming, *Satya* (सत्य) or truthfulness, *Astey* (अस्तेय) or non-stealing, *Brahmacharya* (ब्रह्मचर्य) or moderating the senses / celibacy and *Apigrih* (अपिग्रह) or non-possessiveness.

The *niyams* or personal ethics are *Shauch* (शौच) or self-purification, *Santosh* (संतोष) or contentment, *Tap* (तप) or self-discipline, *Swadhyaya* (स्वाध्याय) or self-study and *Ishwar pranidhan* (ईश्वर प्रणिधान) or complete self-surrender (to God).

Vaisheshik System

The **Vaisheshik system** (वैशेषिक दर्शन) recognises God as the cause of the world and also that the physical world is real. Physical objects exist independent of the mind, but the latter may perceive them differently. All objects are reducible to a finite number of atoms; earth, water, fire, and air are made of indivisible *parmanus* (परमाणु) or atoms. Dust particles visible in the sunbeam are the smallest perceivable particles and are made of three parts, each of which is further defined.

The basic text is the Vaisheshik Sutras of Sage Kanad (कणाद) a disciple of Panchshikha (of Sankhya Philosophy) c. 2nd century BCE. It proclaims the futility of life in the temporary world (*maya*) and proposes that an understanding of god can free an individual from *karm*, following which liberation will ensue; further that the individual souls are eternal and pervade the material body for a (limited) time.

Over the centuries, the school merged with the Nyaya system of Indian philosophy to form the combined school of Nyaya-Vaisheshik. Both these are more or less scientific systems developed to understand God and His Creation simply because we cannot fully test or reproduce both of them in our laboratory systems. These two systems focus on understanding all that we see, observe, feel, think, and experience with our five senses and four levels of *antahkaran* (mind, ego, intellect, consciousness/memory, and emotions). Nyaya is a system of logic or rules whereas Vaisheshik is system of study of the origin and evolution of the universe / its particles (*Kan* कण).

Nyaya System

The Nyaya system (न्याय दर्शन) attempts to prove the existence of God, based on the Veds, and to attain *moksha*. It deals with logic, the process of reasoning. It gives priority to *pramans* (प्रमाण) or valid sources of knowledge (perception, inference, comparison, and testimony) and greatly focuses on methodology. Nyaya Darshan is the basis of all Sanskrit philosophical studies, other systems of Indian philosophy draw on this process. The Nyaya school is based on texts known as the Nyaya Sutras, which were written by Sage Aksapad Gautam (not to be confused with either Buddha or Maharishi Gautam), probably in the second century CE. An important commentary is by Vatsyayan, c.450–500 CE.

Purva Mimansa Philosophy

The (earlier) **Purva Mimansa system** (मीमांसा दर्शन) was founded by Jaimini (जैमिनि) c. 300-200 BCE, and pursues freedom from rebirth through action. It dwells on the ritual aspects of the Veds (mainly the Brahmans). Issues regarding the nature of the universe, nature of soul, the laws of *karm* and the final release from the bondage of *karm* are discussed to form the rational basis of Vedic ritualism. The foundation text here is the Purva Mimansa Sutras of Jaimini which has 12 chapters but its several early commentaries are lost.

Jaimini accepts three proofs or *pramans* - perception (directly from sense-contact, hence related to objects that exist), inference (from the relationship between two things) and *shabd* or testimony (knowledge through words). The focus is not in the existence of God but rather in the character of *dharm,* interpreted for a ritualistic purpose. The aim of Mimansa is to give rules for the interpretation of the Veds, and to provide a philosophical justification for the observance of Vedic ritual. It is based on the *karmkand* portion of the Veds, while the *Uttar Mimansa* is on the *gyankand* portion. It advocates that Vedic rituals and righteous deeds are essential for *dharm.*

By refraining from prohibited deeds and actions inspired by desires, one can be cleansed from sins, leading to a state beyond *dharm* and *adharm.* After experiencing the result of past *karm,* the body dies. If the state beyond *dharm* and *adharm* is attained by then, there is liberation or *Moksh.*

Uttar Mimansa Philosophy

The (later) **Uttar Mimansa** or Vedant philosophy (वेदांत दर्शन) concentrates on the philosophical teachings of the Upanishads. The Brahm sutras (ब्रह्म सूत्र) of Badrayan c. 200-

400 CE, attempt to reconcile the seemingly contradictory and diverse statements of the various Upanishads and the Bhagvad Gita, literally stitching together the various Vedant teachings into a logical and self-consistent whole. However, these *sutras* are reportedly so terse that not only are they capable of being interpreted in multiple ways, they are often incomprehensible without the aid of the various commentaries. The whole system in the Brahm Sutras has been developed in 555 *sutras* that consist mostly of two or three words each.

There are different schools of Vedant. The most well known is **Advait** (अद्वैत) (Nondualism or not two) Vedant which believes in Brahm alone being real and *Nirgun* (निर्गुण) or without attributes. A well-known proponent was Adi Shankaracharya in the 9th century CE. Vivekchudamani (विवेकचूड़ामणि) is a Sanskrit poem attributed to Adi Shankaracharya. It expounds the Advait Vedant philosophy and has 580 verses. It is in the form of a dialogue between an unidentified master and disciple, on the nature of the *Atma* and the steps to reach Brahm. The Vivekchudamani describes developing *vivek* or the faculty of discrimination as essential for *Moksh*. It has covered several of the more important concepts of the Upanishads.

Vishishtadvait (विशिष्टाद्वैत) (Qualified Nondualism) Vedant - the earliest works are no longer available. Ramanuja (11th century CE) was the proponent of *Sagun* (सगुण) Brahm, the concept of Brahm or God, the ultimate power, having a definite form, name and attributes.

The last is **Dvait** (द्वैत) (Dualism) Vedant. Madhav (13th century CE) has authored several works. Here Brahm is identified with Vishnu (Narayan) who is the independent Reality. The other reality is of the Universe and *Prakriti* or matter; the *jivs* or souls are not 'created' by God, nonetheless are entirely dependent on Him for their existence.

Dharm Sutras and Shastras.

The idea of dharm (law, duty, truth), which is central to Hinduism, was expressed in a genre of texts known as the **Dharm Sutras and Shastras**.

The aim of the *sutras* (सूत्र meaning thread) was to reduce the mass of details and to give a simple succinct account (without interpretation) of the rites; thus putting less of a burden on memory – the mode of teaching and learning. There was the utmost brevity, so much so that they frequently became terse, and require commentaries to explain them. As mentioned earlier, the Vedangs included the Kalpa sutras or texts on rituals. Amongst these, the **Shraut** (श्रौत) texts, based on the *Shrutis*, deal with the rites performed by the priests, while **Grihya Sutras**, based on the *Smritis*, are on rituals performed by the householder and his wife and the **Shulba Sutras** deal with construction of the *yagyasthal* or fire arena and have advanced mathematics and geometry.

Dharm Sutras

The **Dharm Sutras**, or "manuals on *dharm*", were texts inspired by the Veds and contain rules of conduct and rites as were practiced in various Vedic schools. The *Dharm Sutras* recognize three sources of *dharm*: revelation (i.e. the Ved), tradition, and good custom. Their principal contents address the duties of people at different stages of life, or *ashrams* (studenthood, householdership, retirement, and renunciation); dietary regulations; offenses and expiations; and the rights and duties of kings.

They discuss purification rites, funeral ceremonies, forms of hospitality, and daily oblations, and even mention juridical matters. The most important of these texts are the sutras of Maharishi Gautam, Baudhayan (800 BCE, also known for his calculations of the square root of 2 and an initial version of Pythagoras theorem etc.), Apastamb Gautam and Vashishth.

Dharm Shastras

The contents of the Dharm Sutras were further elaborated in the more systematic **Dharm Shastras** (धर्मशास्त्र), which in turn became the basis of Hindu law. The Dharm Shastras (law books), though derivatives of earlier Vedic texts such as the Dharmsutras, are traditionally considered as part of the Smritis.

The Dharm Shastra of Manu, also known as the **Manu-smriti** (मनुस्मृति) (c. 200 BCE -200 CE), is the most important and earliest metrical work of the Dharm Shastras with 2,694 verses divided into 12 chapters. It prescribes the obligations of the four social classes (*varns*) at the four stages of life (ashrams), and deals with topics such as the origin of the universe, the definition of *dharm*, initiation and Vedic study, marriage, hospitality and funeral rites, dietary restrictions, pollution and purification, rules for women and wives, royal law, juridical matters, pious donations, rites of reparation, the doctrine of *karm*, the soul, and punishment in hell.

Another important Dharm Shastra is **Yagyavalkya Smriti** (200-500 CE). The text is in the form of a story of Yagyavalkya's teachings to the sages of Mithila about *dharm*. Its 1,013 verses are distributed under the three headings of good conduct, law, and expiation. It is said to have a superior vocabulary and level of sophistication. **Parashar Smriti**, a code of laws given by Parashar, the father of Ved Vyas, is a third well known Dharm Shastra.

The **Dharm Shastra** literature, written in Sanskrit, is said to exceed 5,000 titles, as per the Encyclopedia Britannica.

It can be divided into three categories: (1) *sutras* (terse maxims); (2) s*mritis* (shorter or longer treatises in verses); and (3) *nibandhs* (digests of Smriti verses from various quarters) and *vrittis* (commentaries upon individual Smritis). The *nibandhs* and *vrittis* are juridical works and exhibit considerable skill in harmonizing divergent *sutras* and *smritis*.

The techniques of the Dharm Shastras are mainly to state the ancient text, maxim, or verse, to explain the meaning where obscure, and to reconcile divergent traditions, if necessary by the traditional science of interpretation. Where possible, Dharm shastra permits custom to be enforced, if ascertained and if its terms are not repugnant to the principles of life as understood by Brahmins. Brahmin ethics gave Dharm Shastras their colour and provided a test under which many customs of the people could be administered by Hindu kings.

Other texts

The **Yog Vashishth** is the spiritual teaching imparted by Guru Vashishth to young Shri Ram. Its oldest available manuscript is of the 10th century CE, and revisions to the text are dated between 11th and 14th century CE. Yog Vashishth, also known as Maha Ramayan, Uttar Ramayan, etc. is one of the longest texts after Mahabharat, containing 32,000 *shloks*. It is written in Sanskrit by Valmiki who is also famous for writing the epic Ramayan. Most of the scriptures in Sanatan Dharm were narrated **by** God to His devotees, but the Yog Vashishth is a unique scripture as it is narrated **to** Shri Ram.

It is in the form of replies given by Vashishth, to young Ram's queries regarding philosophical problems of life, death, human suffering etc. Vashishth makes it clear that the problem arises out of confusion between the real and the unreal (or that which is changeable) due to the seeming reality of its appearance. Life is the field where this confusion takes place and life must also be the field where this confusion is corrected.

Three examples found in the Upanishads are frequently mentioned in this book. In the dark, a snake may be imagined and feared, but light (knowledge) will reveal the true nature – that it is actually only a rope lying there. The second is that what is visible is an ornament but when melted its essence is always gold (i.e. the body is temporal, the soul within is the truth). And the third is of the space inside a pot (or a room) –

when the pot or the walls are broken, the space immediately merges with that around and cannot be identified independently – and so it is with our individual *atma* and *parmatma*. (These examples are discussed in greater detail in Part II of this book).

The **Ashtavakra Gita** (अष्टावक्र गीता) is an Advait Vedant scripture said to have been written in the period immediately after the Bhagvad Gita. It is a dialogue between the learned sage Ashtavakra (whose body was deformed in eight places) and Janak, king of Mithila (and the father of Sita), on the nature of soul, reality and bondage. It is aimed at triggering self-realization; there are no suggestions for self-improvement, no rules for moral behaviour, no practical wisdom for daily life. It teaches detachment with no illusion of person. It says "When there is no "I" there is only liberation, when "I" appears bondage appears with it..... Look upon friends, lands, wealth, houses, wives, gifts and all apparent good fortune as a passing show, as a dream lasting three to five days."

The **Yog Yagyavalkya** (योग याज्ञवल्क्य) is a classical treatise on yog traditionally attributed to sage Yagyavalkya. It takes the form of a dialogue between Yagyavalkya and the renowned female philosopher Gargi. Yog (which means addition) is defined as the union between the living Self (*jivatma*) and the supreme Self (*parmatma*). The extant Sanskrit text consists of 12 chapters and contains 504 verses. Several later yog texts on the Hath Yog and the Kundalini Yog make frequent references to this text.

Some other important ancient religious / non-religious texts are also given here.

Ayurved is attributed to Dhanvantari, the physician to the gods, who received knowledge from Brahma (the Creator). Its earliest concepts were set out in Atharva Ved. Other prominent early names are Aitareya and Agnivesh. **Charak Sanhita** (चरक संहिता) is an early text on Ayurved by Charak, a physician. It reportedly reached its present form in the 1st century CE, although there were earlier versions. The extant text is said to have eight sections, totalling 120 chapters. These sections deal with healthy living, collection of drugs and their uses, pathology, various tools of diagnostics & medical studies, fetal generation and anatomy of the human body, diagnosis of disease on the basis of *tridosh*, therapeutics, pharmaceutics and toxicology etc.

The **Sushrut Sanhita** (सुश्रुत संहिता) is by Sushrut, a surgeon who flourished in c. 6th century BCE. He is known for his groundbreaking operations, which include rhinoplasty (the repairing or remaking of a nose), removal of a dead foetus, and lithotomy (surgical incision into hollow organs such as the urinary bladder to remove stones). The Sushrut Sanhita reached its present form by the 7th century CE, and reportedly in its 184 chapters contains descriptions of 1,120 illnesses and 700 medicinal plants. It discusses surgical techniques of the removal of the prostate gland, hernia surgery, caesarean section, management of intestinal obstruction and perforated intestines, the principles of fracture management and fitting of prosthetics. It classifies bones and their reaction to the injuries, and gives a classification of eye diseases including cataract surgery. The *Sanhita* describes eight types of surgical procedures and lays down the basic principles of plastic surgery. Sushrut is reported to be the pioneer of anaesthesia.

Arthashastra is a science of wealth or economics. Its well-known book is **Arthashastra** written around 300 BCE by Chanakya (also known as Kautilya), and deals with governance, and duties and privileges of a ruler. Its scope however is far wider than statecraft, and it offers an outline of the entire legal and bureaucratic framework for administering a kingdom. It has a wealth of descriptive cultural detail on topics such as mineralogy, mining and metals, agriculture, animal husbandry, medicine and the use of wildlife. The Arthashastra also focuses on issues of welfare (for instance, redistribution of wealth during a famine) and the collective ethics that hold a society together.

(Note: In respect of the Smriti texts, two aspects may be kept in mind. First, that Hindu sages believed in knowledge but not in proclaiming their authorship. Second, that the original texts are generally lost and the available information may be through commentaries or bhashyas *on them).*

Estimated Timeline

Various sources give widely varying range of dates for our ancient scriptures, both *Shrutis* and the *Smritis*, frequently differing by several centuries. Any timeline can thus only be an approximation.

Rig Ved : 1500 – 1100 BCE
Sam Ved : 1500 - 500 BCE
Yajur Ved : 1500 - 500 BCE
Atharva Ved : 1500 - 500 BCE
Early Upanishads : 1200 - 500 BCE
Bhagvad Gita : 500 BCE - 200 BCE
Ramayan : 400 BCE - 400 CE
Mahabharat : 400 BCE - 400 CE
Mimansa Sutra : 300-200 BCE
Arthashastra : 400 BCE - 200 CE
Vaisheshik Sutra : 2nd century BCE
Nyaya Sutra : 2nd century CE
Yog Sutras of Patanjali : 100 BCE - 500 CE
Manu-smriti : c. 200 BCE -200 CE
Purans : 3rd - 16th century CE
Yog Vashishth : 11th - 14th century CE

The Upanishads

Introduction

The Upanishads are Hindu scriptures that constitute the *Vedant* or the concluding portion of the Veds. They do not belong to any particular period: the oldest date to the first millennium BCE or even earlier, while the latest were composed in the medieval and early modern period (say from the 5th century CE to the 18th century). It is seen that the timelines are blurred, thus while the *Itihas* (the Ramayan and the Mahabharat) and the *Purans* are considered more recent texts, yet references to these are found even in the older Upanishads.

The Upanishads are a series of brief writings that originated from hymns and teachings in early Indian civilization. Typically, these teachings were an oral tradition that the learned *rishis* passed down to the students seeking truth and knowledge about themselves, their world, and the universe. However, the Upanishads could be stimulating to anyone who shares this quest for meaning.

Just like the other parts of the Veds, these are also *shruti* texts and generally do not have any known author. The Upanishads recognize monistic ideas - the philosophical theory that reality is a unified whole, grounded in a single basic substance or belief, and they attempt to explain everything in terms of a single principle.

Ten to thirteen Upanishads are considered principal or *Mukhya* by various sources; about 108 are recognized as such (though some hold these to be over 200 and counting with many being more recent additions). The Muktika Upanishad, which has the teachings of Shri Ram to his devotee, Hanuman, gives the list of 108 Upanishads.

The *Mukhya* Upanishads form the core of the ancient Upanishad texts. They span the 1st millennium BCE and are generally characterised by the belief that there is one God viz. Brahm. These predate the present classical Hinduism. Brihadaranyak is reportedly the first Upanishad and appeared about three thousand years ago.

The Brihadaranyak and the Chhandogya, which are the longest of the Upanishads, occupy a superior position among the Upanishads. They are perhaps the most complex and discuss profound philosophical truths through numerous anecdotes. They form the basis of the later development of the Vedant philosophy. Of the ten *Mukha* Upanishads taken up in this book, these two, being the most multifaceted, feature in the end.

Scholars and philosophers from both the East and the West acknowledge the Upanishads to be beautiful in poetry and exceptionally rich in philosophy. It is seen however that they do not form a unified pattern of thought and knowledge of Brahm, the sole Reality, is set out in various different ways. The treatment of the subjects is also not methodical and connected but rather loose and scattered. They often use stories and analogies to explain, and almost always follow a *guru – shishya* style, with discourses between teachers and disciples.

Though the principal Upanishads are attached to one or the other Ved *Sanhita* (वेद संहिता), two distinct differences are observable. First, as compared to the *Sanhitas*, in the Upanishads, there is less focus on the deities of Nature and on ritual, and considerably more emphasis on philosophy. Another aspect is that from a multiple of gods, the focus has shifted to the single supreme Brahm (ब्रह्म), who is the Ultimate Reality (these texts do not indicate the trinity of Brahma, Vishnu, Mahesh nor Hanuman, Ganesh, Devi or the gods that we now have in our day-to-day life; these latter gaining prominence from the Puranic literature).

The second difference is that the universe is considered unsubstantial and temporary. The individual soul (*Atma* आत्मा) exists and continues even after death, until it ultimately attains oneness with the Supreme Brahm.

The Upanishads speak of a **universal spirit** (*Brahm*) and of an **individual soul**, (*Atma*). At times they assert the identity of both yet sometimes use the terms interchangeably. Brahm is the ultimate, supreme and unequalled, ingrained or innate, the sum total of all that ever was, is, or shall be. Brahm alone is constant, permanent and eternal - *sat* (सत्); or the only truth that exists.

The mystical nature and intense philosophical bent of the Upanishads has led to their discussion in numerous manners, giving birth to the three main schools of Vedant - Advait, Dvait and Vishishtadvait. The Upanishads also contain revelations of the divine syllable *Aum* or *Om* that underlies all existence.

The Upanishads highlight the various ways and means of attaining Brahm. The principal method is deep inward introspection or direct inward closeness or meditation. Deep thought, with the conviction that one is not different from Brahm, is the great meditational technique. As this meditation is only an affirmation of the knowledge of the universal existence of Brahm, it is also called *gyan* (ज्ञान), the path of wisdom.

While the **Gayatri Mantra** and the **Mritunjay mantra** both come from the *Sanhita* of the Rigved, the Upanishads give us several of our well-known expressions and prayers e.g. **"Om Shantih, Shantih, Shantih", "Satyamev Jayate", "Asto Ma Sadgamaya"** etc.

It is interesting to see that, unlike our present system of examinations where the student is tested on the knowledge acquired, the Upanishads follow a different course. Most learning has to be realised by oneself (self-knowledge) and fitness for learning is gauged by the guru through various tests, usually of austerity and discipline, **before** any wisdom is passed on to the disciple (e.g. in the *Chhandogya, Kath* and

Prashna Upanishads).

The words of the Upanishads cannot be understood in terms of their literal meaning and the passages are to be reflected upon to get a clear understanding. *(Note: In view of the deep study required to understand the Upanishads, this book does not attempt to put forward a discourse on the Upanishads. However, some texts from various translations have been used for retaining a sense of the original character).*

All the Upanishads start with a prayer (the first word of which is *Om*, they also usually end with another prayer. Many of the Upanishads also give the line of teachers of the knowledge, tracing this right back to *Hiranyagarbh* or Brahma the Creator. It is also seen that there is some repetition of mantras or lines amongst the Upanishads.

A few concepts and terms seen across several Upanishads are next discussed.

Some terms and concepts in the Upanishads

*(**Note**: Two aspects of the Upanishads may be kept in mind. First, many terms are introduced or mentioned in one or the other Upanishad which have gained credence in our religion, they are mentioned and explained here to a limited extent so as to bring familiarity with these terms and concepts before reading about the individual Upanishad.*

Second, not all of the Upanishads relate to Brahm as the Supreme, there is also the Prajapati, the Purush, the Atma, etc. While these terms are discussed further on, they more frequently refer to the creator- Brahma, the first created being and the soul respectively).

The Upanishads make a distinction between Brahm without qualities (*Nirgun* निर्गुण) and with qualities (*Sagun* सगुण). *Nirgun* Brahm is incomprehensible, the pure Absolute. *Sagun* Brahm called *Ishvar* is Brahm in the observable (phenomenal) universe and the Self in the individual selves.

Advait and **Dvait**: Some Upanishads hold that there is only one reality — Brahm. Thus philosophical schools such as Advait (non-dualism) see the "spirit" within each living entity as being fully identical with Brahm. Or in simpler terms that the individual *atma* is essentially a part of Brahm and on *moksh* goes back or merges with Brahm. The Self which is of the nature of pure consciousness is constant, real, eternal or *sat* (सत्), while the phenomena constituting the world are constantly changing and therefore unreal or *asat* (असत्).

Some Upanishads however hold the view (of Sankhya philosophy) that reality is split into two: spirit or *purush* (पुरुष), and *prakriti* (प्रकृति) – nature or matter, the latter is without awareness or *jad* (जड़). Schools such as Dvait (द्वैत) or dualism differentiate between the individual *atma* in living beings i.e. *jivatma* (जीवात्मा), and the Supreme *atma* i.e. *Parmatma* (परमात्मा) as being at least partially separate.

Sat (सत्) is the true essence (nature), that which is eternal, and unchangeable. It implies that which is good, true, virtuous, real, existing, enduring, lasting, and essential. In our ancient texts it refers to the Universal Spirit or Being - Brahm. **Asat** (असत्) refers to the opposite of *sat*, that is delusion, distorted, untrue, the fleeting impression that is incorrect, non-existent and false – *maya*, the world etc.

Atma is the ultimate in us, whereas **Brahm** is the ultimate in the cosmos. **Atma** – the essential Self or 'inner-self' of any living being, is the substance of everyone and everything. Thus *atma* refers to the individual spirit. It is ever-free, pure consciousness. When the universal Brahm is conceived as the deepest reality of an individual, it is called the *Atma*. It is the essential Self and not the physical, not the mental, not even the causal sheath of personality all of which get negated in another condition of being– namely deep sleep.

This essential Being also indicates the character of the

Universal Reality. This final substance is constituted of the essence of everything, it is Self, the *Atma*. It (Brahm) is the total substance of all created beings. Even as there cannot be a cause behind the final cause, there cannot be an *Atma* behind the *Atma*; there cannot be anything other than this Universal Reality (Brahm).

The idea of *Atma* and Brahm is illustrated by an oft-quoted analogy—the example of the **limited room space and the unlimited total space**. The atmospheric space is not limited in any manner. Yet we feel that the space inside the four walls of a room is limited; the space in the room, identifying itself with the walls, assumes to itself a special ego or independent status as the room space. The so called room space was the same as the total space before the walls were constructed and if the walls were to be demolished, the former room space will go back to the total space or will be identified with the total space. Thus the room space is actually nothing other than the total space—both are one and the same. (The same concept is sometimes illustrated by the space inside a pot instead of a room).

The empirical world is temporary, changing and hence non-real, an appearance born out of **Maya** (illusion) or nescience–ignorance or *avidya* (अविद्या). The All-pervading Reality, as the *jiv*, identifies with the body, mind and intellect and, in its own delusion or *Maya* considers itself a separate personality. Once this delusion takes place it acquires ideas of its own mortality, egoism, vanity and the consequent misfortunes.

Atma is that Reality which, though eternal, undivided and indivisible, has come to manifest itself within the locus of the body (the analogy of the room space). The undivided Reality is **Brahm**, All-pervading, Absolute and Unborn as in the case of the total space mentioned in the above example. The Mandukya Upanishad declares *ayam atma brahm* or "this *Atma* is Brahm".

The *Jiv* (or being) is ignorance at the individual level; it faces the consequences of one's actions (*karm* कर्म) – right and wrong, good and evil. It creates bondages through action and egoism, and loosens the bonds through intellect or *buddhi* (बुद्धि), the counter force of ignorance.

The philosophy of the Upanishads is that it is ignorance about the existence of the Universe that binds the individual *jiv* to the series of births and deaths. Our sorrows are, in a way, created by our own selves. The ego asserts a reality, independent of what really is. This affirmation of individuality or something distinct, *jivatma,* is the cause of the sorrow or the suffering of the *jiv*. Births and deaths are the consequences to the individual for the false notion that it has about the independence of its own Self.

The **Jiv has four states** of waking, dreaming, deep sleep and *turiya* (तुरीय) and it is in this last state that the *jiv* becomes one with the Supreme Self.

In our scriptures we continually find **the simile of the snake**

and the rope. That is, in darkness we see a rope lying on the ground, assume it is a snake lying there and try to run away out of fear. Yet, when a light is brought we see only a rope. The fear and excitement then vanish within no time. The rope was always real, was always there. The snake was an illusion that existed only in our mind causing all sorts of mental disturbances. Illusion is always a mental phenomenon, never a real or objective thing. So it is illusion and ignorance that we must overcome.

A frequent third illustration is of the **ornament and gold** (or weapon and iron, pot and clay etc.). What is seen is the ornament – the bracelet, but the essence is always the same – gold. And once gold is known, (the essence of) all ornaments are known.

Purush, the dweller in the body, is three-fold: the Outer-Atma or *the Bahyatma* (बहिरात्मा, बाह्यात्मा) which is born and dies; the Inner-Atma or *Antaratma* (अंतरात्मा) comprehends the whole range of material phenomena with which the *Jiv* concerns itself, and the *Parmatma* (परमात्मा) which is all-pervading, unthinkable, indescribable, without action.

(Note: The term Purush in our scriptures has held varied meanings – the original man, a primeval giant with a thousand heads and a thousand feet whose parts when cut up formed the universe; Prajapati the creator; the soul; the origin of the four varns (वर्ण) etc.).

Some Upanishads also mention the term '*Measure of the thumb*' and say that the **Purush** (पुरुष), of the size of the thumb, the inner Self, is always seated in (the lotus of) the heart of all living beings. Hence the Self or the Soul is referred to as the Indweller (incidentally the Upanishads do not ascribe any gender to Brahm or to the term *Purush*).

This "being" dwelling inside the heart has been equated with the *jiv*, the individualistic *jivatma*, or the 'Self', which carries the consciousness and a metaphysical body (the *karan sharir* कारण शरीर or the causal body). The latter accumulates the experiences of the physical, earthly life and carries the information or knowledge acquired during previous births. Thus *jiv* is a spark of divinity, its place in the body is the heart region, and it is born again and again till it becomes detached from the *karan sharir* (the Causal body).

The word **Prajapati** means the Lord or Father of all that exists. It is like a designation in an organization, a post to which someone is promoted. *Prajapati* is also called *Hiranyagarbh* (हिरण्यगर्भ) or *Brahma* - the Creator, (not to be confused with Brahm the Supreme Being). According to Vedant, everything, including *Prajapati* comes from Brahm or is projected from Brahm. Brahm does not create anything because he is *nirgun* and *nirakar* (निर्गुण, निराकार) i.e. without qualities and without form.

Sansar (संसार) is the repeating cycle of birth, life and death (re-birth), as well as one's actions and consequences in the past, present, and future. The current life is only one of many — stretching back before birth into past existences and reaching forward beyond death into future lives. During the course of each life, the quality of the actions (*karm*) performed determines the future destiny. There is no beginning to this cycle but it can be ended with a realisation of the identity of Self. The aim is to realize this truth, the achievement of which is **moksh** (मोक्ष) or the coming out of the cycle of birth, life and death.

Ishavasyopanishad or Ish Upanishad (Shukla Yajur Ved)

The Ishavasya Upanishad (ईशावास्य or ईश उपनिषद, ईशोपनिषद) is one of the shortest of the Upanishads, more like a brief poem, consisting of 18 verses or *shloks* (श्लोक), and constitutes the final chapter of the *Sanhita* of the Shukla Yajurved.

The first verse of the Ish Upanishad is considered particularly important and translates to:

> *"Enveloped by the Lord must be This All — each thing that moves on earth.*
> *With that renounced enjoy thyself. Covet no wealth of any man."*[2]

Or - *He pervades all this world that wakes. Enjoy what He has given and do not desire the wealth of others.*

The Ish Upanishad starts with Brahm Vidya, and is significant for its description of the nature of the "Supreme Being" as one (the Self) who moves yet it moves not, who is far and is near, and who although fixed and unmoving is swifter (than the mind), the senses (the other deities) cannot reach it, for it proceeds ahead; remaining static it overtakes others that run; it is within all and it is without all.

---

[2] www.sacred-texts.com

The Upanishad touches on the paths of knowledge and of action. Both action (without any expectation of its fruit) and knowledge (of Self) together are essential to attain Brahm; either of them alone leads to Darkness (i.e. death and rebirth, not knowledge of Brahm and hence *moksh* and immortality).

The Upanishad also states that the wise man beholds all beings in the Self and the Self in all beings; for that reason he does not hate anyone; all things have become the Self. There cannot be any sorrow for him who beholds that oneness.

The invocation or opening prayer, which today is an oft-recited mantra, is: *Om purnamadah purnamidam purnaat purnamudachyate, purnasya purnamaadaya purnamevaavashishyate, Om Shantih Shantih Shantih.* (ॐ पूर्णमदः पूर्णमिदं पूर्णात् पूर्णमुदच्यते, पूर्णस्य पूर्णमादाय पूर्णमेवावशिष्यते. ॐ शांतिः शांतिः शांतिः)

Meaning thereby (on the Supreme Being) "The whole is all That. The whole is all This. The whole was born of the whole. Taking the whole from the whole, what remains is the whole."[3] (This prayer is also found in the Brihadaranyak Upanishad). The Upanishad concludes with a prayer to Surya to give knowledge, and to Agni to destroy the sins of *karm* (कर्म).

---

[3] www.sivanandaonline.org

Ken Upanishad (Sam Ved)

The Ken Upanishad (केन उपनिषद, केनोपनिषद) (*'Ken'*, meaning 'by whom') is from the Sam Ved and has four sections, the first two in verse and the other two in prose. The portion in verse sings the meditation of Brahm, the controller and mover of senses - *Not that which the eye can see, but that whereby the eye can see; Not that which the ear can hear, but that whereby the ear can hear; Not that which speech can illuminate, but that by which speech can be illuminated; Not that which the mind can think, but that whereby the mind can think; Not that which the pran (प्राण) can breathe but by which the pran can breathe: know that to be Brahm the eternal, and not what people here adore.*

The Upanishad goes on to say that if anyone thinks they know Brahm well, actually know little of Brahm's true nature. A person who thinks she does not know Brahma fully, yet cannot say that she does not know him, knows Him. He comes to the thought of those who know him beyond thought, not to those who imagine he can be attained by thought.

The prose part of the Upanishad shows that all the gods / deities have no power of their own but derive their strength from Brahm and to this effect it then narrates a tale. The deities had won a victory over evil forces which they thought was theirs rather than due to the power of the Absolute Brahm. Brahm appeared before them as a spirit (*yaksh*) whom Agni and Vayu challenged saying they had the power to burn all things or blow away all that is on earth. But they were unable to burn or blow even the straw placed before them. The gods then asked Indra to find out who the *yaksh* was. Finally before Indra stands Uma (representing knowledge) who reveals that the spirit is the Absolute Brahm, and that it was through Him that the gods had attained victory. Thereafter, Indra who first learnt of the Supreme Spirit, and Agni and Vayu who had also approached the spirit and learnt it to be Brahm, became superior to the other gods.

Whether it is the flash of lightning or the wink of the eyes or the thinking of the mind, all of the power that is shown is the power of Brahm and for this reason, at all the times, meditation should be on Brahm.

The Ken Upanishad concludes that austerity, restraint, and action are the foundation of the knowledge of Brahm; the Veds are its limbs, and truth is its home. The one who knows it is freed from sin and becomes established in the infinite and highest heaven.

Kath Upanishad (Krishna Yajur Ved)

Kath Upanishad (कठ उपनिषद, कठोपनिषद) belongs to the Krishna Yajur Ved. It is one of the most widely known Upanishads and has some passages common to the Gita.

It employs the story of a father Vajshravas (वाजश्रवस) who, desirous of attaining heaven, performs a *yagya* wherein he is required, amongst other things, to give away all his worldly possessions. His son Nachiketa (नचिकेता) observes that even cows that were too old and unfit for any use were being given away (to the priests), these were unworthy gifts and could not bring anything but misery and sorrow to his father. He asks to whom he was given (since he too was a possession of his father). On repeated questioning Vajshravas, in irritation, says that he (Nachiketa) has been given to *Yam* (यम), the god of Death.

Nachiketa goes to the abode of *Yam*, but not finding him there, waits for Yam who returns after three days. Concerned about the discourtesy shown to Nachiketa, Yam offers him three boons, one for each night that Nachiketa had spent waiting. Nachiketa asks to be given knowledge about life after death. With worldly desires and delights, wealth and power, *Yam* first tests and satisfies himself on Nachiketa's sincerity and fitness for knowledge.

Yam's teachings concerning true immortality begin by distinguishing between *prey* (प्रेय) or what is pleasant, and *shrey* (श्रेय) or what is beneficial – the path of pleasure and ignorance as against the path of joy and wisdom. Both attract the *Jiv,* but the wise man analyses and understands the difference between them. The one who follows the *shrey* path attains good results here and in the hereafter, while the one who is interested only in earning wealth or in other worldly pleasures, takes on the *prey* path, loses control of himself and of his spiritual progress, and goes from death to death.

It goes on to say that what lies beyond right and wrong, beyond past and future, the Word that all the Veds glorify is *Aum* or *Om* (ॐ). One who has understood *Om* is neither born again nor dies. Concealed in the heart of all beings is the *Atma.* The inner Self or *Atma* is eternal, everlasting, neither perishable nor changeable; it is not destroyed by the destruction of the body. It is smaller than the small and greater than the great, sitting it goes far and sleeping it goes everywhere.

Just as the sun, which is the eye of the entire world, is not tainted by the external impurities seen by the eyes, so also the indwelling Self of all beings, though one, is not tainted by the sorrows of the world. The *Atma* cannot be reached even through deep knowledge, unless evil ways are abandoned, there is rest in the senses, concentration in the mind and peace in one's heart. A few beautiful lines on *Atma,* from this Upanishad are given at the end of this book.

The Kath Upanishad includes the oft-quoted *Rath Kalpana* - the analogy of a chariot. *Atma* or the Self is the master of the chariot, the body is the chariot itself, intellect (*buddhi*) or reason is the charioteer, the mind are the reins, the ten senses (the five organs of perception viz. ear, skin, eye, tongue, nose, and the five organs of action viz. voice, legs, arms, reproductive organs, evacuating organs) are the chariot horses, and the objects perceived by the senses are the road pursued by them.

In increasing order of superiority they are senses, objects, mind, intellect and Self. Those whose intellect is distracted and mind uncontrolled, their senses are undisciplined like vicious horses, and they go on to re-birth. The senses are outward-going, they go to the world outside not to the Spirit within. The wise look within and find their own Self, see Him in their souls and attain peace and joy eternal. The wise and the disciplined obtain their goal and are freed from the cycle of rebirth.

The *Purush* (or the *Atma*), who is of the size of one's thumb, resides in the center of one's body (within the cave of heart) and is like a flame without a smoke, crystal-clear. If one is unable to understand the true Self before death, the *Jiv*, based on actions thoughts and knowledge he had during his lifetime, is born again with bodies, human or as plants. The *Purush* is pure, eternal and immortal, Brahm.

The *Atma* multiplies its single form and entering various bodies, takes on various forms and, although it remains as one and the same, it exists even beyond all objects within which it is present. Those wise men who perceive the *Atma* are entitled to eternal peace, not the others.

The mind is beyond the senses. Beyond it is the brain or intuition. Beyond that is the great soul (one of the aspects of the *Atma*). Beyond that great soul is the non-manifested or the invisible (or the Supreme Divine called as the *avyakta* - अव्यक्त). Above the non-manifested is the *Purush* (the all-knowing and all-pervading *Atma*). He is devoid of any particular mark or characteristic.

The *Atma* is beyond sound and form, without touch and taste and smell, eternal and unchanging, without beginning and end, even beyond reasoning. It (Brahm) is not attainable by speech, mind or eyes, it cannot be obtained otherwise than by saying that it exists. When consciousness of the *Atma* manifests itself, on knowing Him to be so, the *Jiv* is liberated and attains immortality. If a man is able to realise Brahm here before giving up his body, he is liberated; if not, he is embodied again into the world. When all desires that dwell in the heart are destroyed, then the mortal becomes immortal and enjoys Brahm even here.

Thus Nachiketa, having obtained knowledge, attained Brahm and became liberated and free from death.

Mundak Upanishad (Atharva Ved)

The Mundak Upanishad (मुण्डक उपनिषद्), which belongs to the Atharva Ved, has 64 verses and is on Brahm Vidya (knowledge of Brahm). *Mund* means to shave – the teachings shave or liberate from error and ignorance. The conversation here is between the Angiras (representing the disciples of Atharva, the son of Brahma the Creator), and Shaunak (representing the householder or the student-*rishi*).

This Upanishad distinguishes between *Para Vidya* (परा विद्या) or the higher knowledge of the Supreme Brahm and *Apara Vidya* (अपरा विद्या) or the lower knowledge of the four Veds and of phonetics, ritual, grammar, definition, metrics, and astrology (i.e. the six Vedangs). It says that rituals of worship and good deeds described in the Veds, took place in the *Treta Yug,* and are practiced to produce good *karm* and yield good fruits. Those who perform rituals of worship and humanitarian works are ignorant and do not know any higher good. After enjoying, in heaven, a suitable sojourn as the reward gained by good works, they enter this world again.

Para Vidya is concerned with Brahm and can eradicate ignorance in its entirety. It is by this higher wisdom and not by sacrifices / *yagyas* or worship (which are considered frail boats), that one can reach Brahm and overcome the cycle of re-birth. Like the Kath Upanishad, the Mundak Upanishad warns against "the ignorance of thinking oneself learned and going around deluded like the blind leading the blind". Only a *sanyasi* or ascetic who has given up everything can obtain the highest knowledge.

This Upanishad describes Brahm in detail – the Self-luminous and formless *Purush*, dwelling within all and without all, unborn, pure, greater than the greatest, without *pran*, without mind. Brahm is the source - from him everything is born - breath, mind, sky, rain, and food etc. All that exists is held in the Mind of God, for they are His thoughts made visible or tangible. He is the innermost Self of all. The universe is not God's creation, but His manifestation.

The deathless Self meditated upon
Himself and projected the universe
As evolutionary energy.
From this energy developed life, mind,
The elements, and the world of karma,
Which is enchained by cause and effect.[4]

It further says that all creatures descend from him as do devotional chants, scriptures, rites, divisions of time, the doer and the deed, gods of diverse descent, angels, men, beasts, birds; from him austerity and meditation, faith, truth, continence, and law. From him spring the organs of sense, their activities, and their objects, together with their awareness of these objects, the seas and the mountains, the herbs and other life-sustaining elements. Brahm is all in all. He is action, knowledge, goodness supreme. He is the

---

[4] The Upanishads by Eknath Easwaran

principle of life, he is speech, and he is mind, he is real and he is immortal.

This Self, who understands all, who knows all, and whose glory is manifest in the universe, lives within the lotus of the heart and is known by the pure in heart. To know him is to untie the knot of ignorance even during this life on earth. He is ever present in the hearts of all, the refuge of all and the supreme goal. Subtler than the subtlest, in whom exists all the worlds and all those that live therein—he is the imperishable Brahm. The wise know him by the power of meditation.

A beautiful simile is of the bow and arrow – *Om* (or the Upanishad or knowledge) is the bow, Self the arrow sharpened with worship (*upasana*), drawn with a concentrated mind towards Brahm the target. During *Moksh*, elements building the body and mind go back to their sources and the Self becomes one with Brahm in the same manner as rivers lose their name and form once they enter the ocean.

The concluding Chapter of the Upanishad explains *Parmatma* and the *Jivatma* – the Supreme Self and the individual Self – their unity and their distinction, and their relationship with each other.

A well-known example is of **two birds sitting on the tree** (heart), inseparable companions, one eats fruits and is filled with sorrow till he looks at the other—who is only looking on as witness – and sees the latter as the Supreme. The individual Self and the Cosmic Self exist in an eternal relation, in a state of perpetual union, in the same place and are inseparable. The two Selves have the identical name or designation, and exist in an identical manner, in companionship and friendship, indicating the deep personal relationship between the *Jivatma* and *Parmatma*. The tree represents the body and the *Jivatma,* who experiences the effects of worldliness, is the bird that tastes the fruits i.e. is engaged in actions that produce consequences both favourable and unfavourable. The *Jivatma's* propensity to be selfish about objects, people and actions takes it deeper and deeper in the unending currents of birth and death.

The other bird is the inner Supreme Self that neither enjoys nor grieves but remains as a mere witness to the acts of the first bird. After experiencing the sweetness and bitterness of the world, the individual Self realizes that it always is the immortal Absolute Self, full of bliss and consciousness and that all along it remained under wrong notions that were tying it down to ignorance about the correct meaning of worldly existence.

As long as a seeker has the concept of being separate from the Self, there exists an ego-centre in him. The moment he realizes that his real nature is divine, his ego vanishes, and he loses his identity. He experiences Pure Consciousness and becomes one with the Eternal *Purush.* Just as the flowing rivers come to an end in the sea and lose their names and forms, so the wise become free from name and form and attain the divine person who is greater than the great.

The concept of Duality and Unity, and the reconciliation of observing the many with knowing the One True Self, is seen repeatedly throughout the Upanishads. The Mundak Upanishad asserts that by realizing that you are the Self, the Supreme source of light, the supreme source of love, you transcend the duality of life and enter into the unitive state.

> *You cannot have the knowledge of the Supreme Soul by means of reasoning, erudition, or studying of the Shrutis;*
> *Only through causeless mercy does He reveal His own person unto him whom He does accept as His own[5]*

Chapter 3 of the Mundak Upanishad has the phrase **Satyamev jayate** or "Truth alone prevails", the national motto of India appearing in the national emblem having four lions.

---

[5] www. shuddhabhakti.com

Prashna Upanishad (Atharva Ved)

The Prashna Upanishad (प्रश्न उपनिषद्, प्रश्नोपनिषद्) belongs to the Brahman portion of the Atharva Ved, it has 67 mantras and deals with six questions put to *rishi* Pippalad by his various disciples. After a year of their studentship, Pippalad answers.

The first question was on the origin of all created beings or where do all beings come from. Pippalad answers that all created beings originated from *Prajapati* (प्रजापति - or the deity presiding over procreation) who manifested himself into many. The many objects we observe in the universe are all really one, which can be classified into the cause and the effect—*pran* (प्राण) or energy (sun, life, fire) and *rayi* (रयि) or matter (food, earth, moon).

The sun is *vaishvanar* (वैश्वानर)–Self, or one who is identified with all living beings, and is *visvarup* or one who assumes all forms. It rises everyday as *Pran* (life) and *Agni* (fire, energy). All that have form or are gross (*sthool* स्थूल) as also all that is formless or subtle (*sukshm* सूक्ष्म) is matter i.e. matter does not mean only solid things which have form but includes even those which do not have forms such as all our thoughts and ideas, sound waves, air, water etc. – even the subtler planes of existence up to Intellect are matter. Hence matter may exist from the grossest to the subtlest.

The apparent duality of *pran* and *rayi* is the visible

characteristic of the world which we are able to observe and experience. If the path of rituals / sacrifices and good actions has been followed *Jivs*, after death, take the *pitri* path or the path of the forefathers when, following a sojourn in Heaven, they return again or are re-born. Those seeking Self through austerity, studentship, devotion and knowledge have no return.

Duality is the very basis of creation and exists in everything in the universe, even in the flow of Time. For example, a year has the duality of the sun moving in the northern and southern hemispheres (*uttarayan* and *dakshinayan)*; a month has the duality of bright and dark fortnights (*Shukla paksh* and *Krishna paksh*); a day of the week has the duality of day and night.

The second question was who / how many *Devs* protect and guard created beings and who among them is supreme? Pippalad discusses how the physical being is kept united and integrated, as also the activities of the body. He says that the deities are the instruments of knowledge (*gyanendriyas*) called the sense organs, and the instruments of action (*karmendriyas*) in the body (space, air, fire, water, earth, speech, mind, eye and ear etc.). They are fully supported by our mind and intellect but *pran* is the chief, the supporter and enlighter of all creatures.

There is then the story of how the *Devs* or the various organs of the body started a controversy amongst themselves, each claiming that it alone supports the body and that without it the body will disintegrate and collapse. *Pran*, divided into five, supports the body and this was accepted by the other *Devs* / organs when they realised that on *pran* departing the body they would also have to depart.

The third question seeks further clarification on *Pran* – its origin, the entrance, functioning and departure from the body as also its importance both at individual and universal levels. Pippalad explains that *Pran* comes from the Self or *Atma*. Just as the shadow originates from the person but does not exist independently, *Pran* the protector of the body originates from the *Atma* (soul), it comes to the body by *Atma's* will (mind, desire) and dividing into five forms, performs various functions in the body.

Pran (प्राण, sun), located in the nose, performs the function of respiration and moves the eyes, ears, nose and mouth. *Apan* (अपान, earth) located in the organs of generation and excretion, performs the function of evacuation or excretion of wastes.

Vyan (व्यान, air) moves in the entire body and performs the function of circulation – it pervades the nerves / channels in the body and gives power and energy to all the limbs and senses to perform their functions. It moves the channels (*nadis*) of the heart (101 channels each divided into 100 branch channels and each of these further sub-divided into 72000 subsidiary branches).

Saman (समान space) located in the central region of the body digests food and kindles the seven fires (two eyes, two ears, two nostrils and one tongue in the mouth) enabling the soul to have the experience of forms, sounds, smells and flavours.

Udan or *Tej* (उदान light, fire) located in the throat maintains heat in the body, moves upwards and departs after death. There are *nadis* (subtle channels of energy) in the heart in which *Pran* in the form of *Udan* circulates. When a person dies his physical body disintegrates, but the power or strength of his sense organs or *pranic* vitality withdraws from these centres and become united with the subtle body, the mind.

The subtle body is conveyed to its next field of activity (for rebirth in another body) by the energy called *udan*. Through one of the *nadis (Sushumna-nadi* सुषुम्ना नाड़ी), *Udan* carries life to heaven or hell based on the good deeds (*punya*) done or sins (*paap*) committed, and to earth (human world) if both *paap* and *punya* are present. Whatever are one's thoughts (at the time of death), that thought remains with the outgoing *pran* and leads to whatever world has been conceived (in the last thoughts).

Thus Pippalad has described the five kinds of pran as:

Main *Pran* — in the eyes, ears, mouth and nose
Apan — downward force, in the organs of sex and excretion
Saman — the equalizing force in the middle digests food
Vyan — distributor of energy, moves through vital currents,

radiating from the heart, where the Self lives
Udan — runs upward through the spinal channel, leads the selfless up the long ladder of evolution, and the selfish down.

The fourth question is on the senses that operate in the three stages - the waking, dreaming and sleeping. The *rishi* explains that the way all rays of the sun go back into sun at the time of sunset, so all the senses of man go back into the mind i.e. become dormant so one does not see or hear etc. during sleep. But still the five *Prans* (*Vyan*, *Upan* etc.) are awake.

The one who sees the dream is the mind (not the *Atma*). In dreams, that deity, the mind, experiences glory. Whatever has been seen or not seen, heard or not heard and whatever is real or not real - he sees it all; he sees all, himself (the mind) being all. During dream-less deep sleep or *sushupti* (सुषुप्ति) even the mind is at rest and everything merges into Self or *Atma;* since all thoughts and desires are lost the 'sleeper' alone is the Lord, the *jivatma* attains bliss. However it goes back into the world on awakening.

When the outside world and dream world are taken away from the mind, what remains is only consciousness and man is said to have reached the dreamless deep sleep state. In this state man is nearest to the Self. In the fourth or final stage – *turiya* (तुरीय), all the factors related to our physical, mental and intellectual personalities retire and there is oneness with the Supreme Reality - *Akshar*, or Brahm.

The fifth question is on worshipping or meditating on *Om*. Pippalad's response is on *Apara* Brahm or Lower Brahm, being *Sagun* i.e. with attributes and known with *apara vidya*. The Supreme Brahm, also called *Para* Brahm or Higher Brahm, is known with *para vidya,* and is *Nirgun*, i.e. devoid of all characteristics and cannot be known through words or thought.

Om or *AUM,* which is the symbol of both the lower and the higher (*Sagun* and *Nirgun*) Brahm, indicates supreme reality, the Parabrahm. By meditating on any part, A, U, M (which are the three stages of consciousness – waking, dream and deep sleep) one attains increasing higher levels, but meditation on all three in totality is meditation on Brahm. The silence or the imperceptible sound in between two successive chants of *AUM* is the fourth state of *turiya* and where one merges into Parabrahm.

The sixth question is - Where is that Supreme Being, the Person of sixteen forms? Pippalad explains that *Purush*, though without any parts, appears to have parts, and resides in the inner body (heart).

The sixteen divine attributes are sixteen parts within the body. The order of evolution of the sixteen parts or *kalas* (कला), the manifestations of the Self or *Purush*, are: 1. Life Principle, *Pran*, 2. Faith, *Shraddha* 3-7. Five Elements, space, air, fire, water and earth 8. Five senses of perception and five organs of action considered as one 9. Mind, 10. Food, 11.

Vigor, 12. Self-discipline, *Tap* 13.Worship or prayers, mantra, 14.Work, *karm* 15.Wisdom, or spiritual worlds representing different states of consciousness, and 16.Name or a distinct identity.

The sixteen parts are created through ignorance or *avidya*. These created entities are unreal, like the objects seen in a dream. After the destruction of *avidya* they again merge in the *Purush* losing their names and forms. Just as the rivers flow towards and are ultimately absorbed in the sea, so these 16 *kalas* (or parts) go towards the Self, and disappear into the *Purush*. After having reached Him, their names and forms get merged and ultimately become one with *Purush*. The Supreme Being thus resides right here, inside the body.

Mandukya Upanishad (Atharva Ved)

The Mandukya Upanishad (माण्डूक्य उपनिषद, माण्डूक्योपनिषद) is the shortest of the Upanishads and belongs to the Atharva Ved. The Upanishad contains twelve verses in prose and is a description of the principle of *Aum (Om)*. It starts by saying "*Ayam atma brahm*" (अयम् आत्मा ब्रह्म) or I am this Self (*Atma*) that is Brahm. Unlike other Upanishads, here there is no tale (of guru-disciple), only a discourse on the symbol AUM whose three elements, A, U, M, may be used to experience the soul itself.

It says that the entire world of objects that humans were aware of in the past, are aware of in the present, and may be aware of in the future, has an unchanging core in all three periods of time, which is represented by the symbol, sound and the word AUM. It goes on to say that if anything can be conceived to exist beyond these three periods of time that also is AUM. Pure Consciousness is AUM, and its four aspects are the four levels of consciousness.

The three sounds A-U-M (ah, ou, mm) and the three letters A, U, M are identical with the three states of waking, dreaming, and sleeping. Yet there is a fourth part of Om or AUM, as the A, U and M, merge into silence. This represents a fourth state, *Turiya* (तुरीय), which is to be realized only in the silence behind and beyond the other three states. It is above feelings and thoughts, a state of pure awareness where all activity ceases.

The first - the sound "A" is the waking state – *vaishvanar* (वैश्वानर) or fire. It is that consciousness which is aware of objects other than oneself, is turned outward to the external world and is the enjoyer of gross material objects - sound, touch, shape or forms, taste and smell—through the respective sense organs. One who knows this sound and this letter, attains the first level of reality, has fulfilment of all longings and is successful.

The second – the sound "U" is dreaming - *tejas* (तैजस) or light. It is the consciousness whose sphere of activity is the dream, which is turned towards the inner world / conscious of internal objects and is the enjoyer of subtle (सूक्ष्म) objects based on the impressions of past experience and mental thoughts. One who knows this state, which is between the two (the preceding "A" or waking, and the succeeding "M" or deep sleep states), attains superior knowledge and equilibrium, and all the successors in his family will be knowers of Brahm.

The third—the sound "M" is deep or dreamless sleep – *pragya* (प्रज्ञा) or knowledge or intellect. It is the consciousness where there is no desire for any gross or subtle object, and all experiences have receded or merged—the state of deep sleep (*sushupti*) is characterized by the absence of knowledge of physical reality. It contains the other two, is that from which the other two states emerge, and into which they recede or merge. Here, one can find the way to clearer knowledge of the two preceding states and experience bliss -

this bliss however is not infinite as it ends upon awakening. A knower of this more subtle state realizes the real nature of the world, and also comprehends all within himself.

The fourth state—the silence after "A-U-M" is that of being one with the soul - *turiya* (तुरीय) is neither sleep nor dream and has no knowledge—internal, intermediate or deep, is beyond this, peaceful and blissful. In this fourth state, consciousness is neither turned outward nor inward, nor both outward and inward; it is beyond both cognition or awareness and the absence of cognition. It is unseen (by sense organs) and is not comprehended through the senses or by the mind. With the cessation of all phenomena, even of bliss, this soundless aspect becomes known.

This fourth state of *Turiya* cannot be experienced through the senses or known by comparison, deductive reasoning or inference; it is indescribable, incomprehensible, and unthinkable with the mind. This is Pure Consciousness itself. It is within the cessation of all phenomena. It is serene, tranquil, filled with bliss, and is one without second. This is the real or true Self that is to be realized. One with direct experience of this expands to Universal Consciousness.

This Upanishad explains the *Nirakar* (निराकार) or the formless, impersonal or attributeless aspect of God and is said to be the only Upanishad that truly defines the *Nirakar* Brahm. (*Note: Several verses in this Upanishad are common to the Prashna Upanishad*).

Taittiriya Upanishad (Krishna Yajur Ved)

The Taittiriya Upanishad (तैत्तिरीय उपनिषद्) is a part of the Krishna Yajur Ved and is constituted by the seventh, eighth and ninth chapters of Taittiriya Aranyak. Regarded as a source-book of the Vedant philosophy, it gives an overview of the entire Ved and includes the essential content of both the *karmkand* and *gyankand*. The Taittiriya Upanishad is divided into three sections or *vallis* (वल्ली).

The *Shiksha Valli* contains prayers to the deities for the removal of obstacles while pursuing spiritual wisdom. It teaches meditation on the names and forms of Brahm, which leads to knowledge and the attainment of all desires. This is the section on instruction and teaches the world to be a combination of various elements and qualities – letter, sound, symbol, emphasis, equality and union; world, light, knowledge creation, body; and *Bhuh, Bhuvah, Suvah and Maha* denoting earth, sky, heaven and Brahm.

It gives the essence of the *karmkand* of the Veds in terms of disciplines, rituals, mantras, meditations, values, code of conduct for daily life, etc. Thus the teacher first instructs the disciple on the significance of the Vedic texts and then regarding conduct of life—to speak the truth and walk in *dharm* or righteousness, not to neglect study, to have children and continue the family line, not to neglect the welfare or duties to gods and fathers. Mother, father and a guest be considered a god; to give with faith, grace, modesty, willingness and friendliness.

It describes the heart as the dwelling-place of Brahm and also the *Sushumna Nadi*, through which lies the path for the attainment of *Sagun Brahm*. The result of such attainment is the enjoyment of self-rule and peace.

It teaches meditation through the symbols of fivefold sets of objects (space, air, fire, water, earth; then matter, life, mind, intelligence, bliss etc.). These objects are both in the outside world and in the body, the two should be contemplated as identical with each other; together they constitute the universe, which is a manifestation of Brahm. This meditation on Brahm through concrete symbols is for inferior students. It then teaches meditation for superior students through the symbol AUM.

A person acquires theoretical knowledge of the scriptures but in order to obtain direct knowledge of Brahm such theoretical knowledge has to be put in practice through the discharge of duties and obligations according to one's *Dharm*. It emphasizes the performance of various duties. A student may attain knowledge of Brahm by meditating on AUM but must not, on that account, neglect the study of the scriptures and compliance with his various other social duties. The students returning home (on the completion of their studies) are told to embrace the householder's life which is the proper place for the discharge of worldly duties.

The other two sections of the Upanishad, give the essence of the *gyankand* of the Ved, in terms of knowledge of *jiv, jagat* and *jagdishswar* followed by the step-by-step process of contemplation on Brahm leading ultimately to *moksh*. In the first chapter the students were initiated into different methods of concentration in pursuit of Brahma Vidya. The teacher now leads them into the process of Self-Discovery.

The *Brahmanand Valli* teaches that *Jiv* consists of food, *pran,* mind, knowledge and bliss as Brahm, and that mediation on them leads to the Supreme goal and Brahm. This section describes the Self as the cause of *akash* or ether, air, fire, water and earth which constitute the body and the world.

(Note: The Upanishads count akash *(आकाश) as one of the five elements and this is translated by most authors as ether, not as sky.* Akash *or ether can be best explained as the all-pervasive life principle or space of the universe, a universal medium in which every single thing is contained, touched and surrounded by. It fills all space and penetrates all matter – it is the fifth and subtlest element).*

The Upanishad speaks of Brahm as Reality (*satya* सत्य), Knowledge (*gyan* ज्ञान) and Infinity (*anant* अनन्त). Although Brahm is a man's inmost Self, he is not conscious of it because the *Atma* or the Self is hidden by five sheaths (*panchkosh*) created by ignorance, these start from the grossest – the physical man, going through the others of mind and intellect to that of bliss.

The outermost sheath of the bodily self, the gross physical sheath produced from food we eat, is the *annamay kosh* – food or matter. The next is the *pranmay kosh* – *pran*, vital breath, the third is the *manomay kosh* – mind or will, the fourth the *vigyanmay kosh* – intellect or wisdom or capacity to know and the fifth, the *anandmay kosh* – bliss. These five sheaths constitute the gross body (*sthool sharir - annamay kosh)*, the subtle body (*sukshm sharir - the pranmay, manomay* and the *vigyanmay kosh*) and the causal body (*karan sharir - anandmay kosh*) of a living creature.

Thereafter the discussion is on food, *pran*, mind and knowledge, and on Brahm as the goal of knowledge.

Brahm is the innermost reality which is untouched by any of the sheaths. Brahm is real as the phenomenal universe consisting of entities, whether with or without form, cannot exist in the absence of a support or cause. Brahm dwells in the hearts of all as consciousness, and is manifest in all acts of reasoning, perception and understanding. The Upanishad describes Brahm as the material and efficient cause of the universe and the essence of all things. It is causeless, being the cause of everything, is itself without a cause.

Worldly happiness is merely a reflection of the bliss of Brahm. Even the highest worldly happiness is produced by external factors and depends upon certain actions on the part of the enjoyer, from Brahma down to man. But the bliss of Brahm lies beyond the highest worldly happiness and is experienced by those who have realized their identification with the Supreme Spirit. The bliss of Brahm does not have higher or lower degrees.

The knower of Brahm attains fearlessness and is not tormented by the illusion of good and evil which are produced by ignorance. When ignorance is destroyed, both good and evil, like all other phenomenal categories, merge in Brahm.

The *Bhrigu Valli* deals with the story of Bhrigu, son of Varun, who receives instructions on Brahm from his father. Brahm is defined as the cause of the creation, continuance and dissolution of the universe. The body and sense-organs are channels for the knowledge of Brahm. Brahm is then described as the physical universe, as the *pran*, the mind, the intellect and finally as Bliss. Bhrigu ultimately discovers that Brahm alone is real and everything else is merely superimposed on it.

This Upanishad also describes the importance of food and teaches various forms through which one can meditate on Brahm. It teaches that by austerity and meditation on each of the elements (of Brahm - food, *pran*, mind, knowledge, bliss) one attains knowledge of the Supreme Self.

Aitareya Upanishad (Rig Ved)

The Aitareya Upanishad (ऐतरेय उपनिषद्) is a short prose text of 33 verses, comprising the fourth, fifth and sixth chapters of the second book of the Aitareya Aranyak of the Rig Ved. It deals with the genesis of the universe and the creation of life, the senses, the organs and the organisms. It also delves into the identity of the intelligence that allows us to see, speak, smell, hear and know.

The first chapter describes the creation from Consciousness. It uses the word 'Brahm' for universal Consciousness and *'Atma'* for individual Consciousness, yet the two being the same are also used interchangeably. *Atma* alone exists as the sole Reality prior to the creation of all names and forms. Creation is the spontaneous act of the Creator, a projection of creator's thoughts, not impelled by any desire or necessity.

The Upanishad begins by describing the creation from Consciousness – it identifies Consciousness as the first cause of creation. There was one Self or *Atma* alone at first and he created the four worlds viz. *Ambh* (अम्भ) or light – above heaven - the water bearing clouds, *Marichi* (मरीचि) or Sun's rays – sky – the world of solar rays, *Mar* (मर) or death – earth – the world of mortals, and *Apah* (आप:) or water – what is below – the world of waters.

He then created the gods for their protection. From water,

he created the *Virat Purush* (विराट पुरुष) to whom he gave the shape of man and endowed him with sense organs and senses, and created their gods, and hunger and thirst.

Then came animals (cow, horse), and the human, and this form (and not that of the cow or the horse) pleased the gods. The various deities entered the body of man through the various organs, along with hunger and thirst. He then created food which tried to run away, the human tried to catch the food by speech, breath, eye, ear, skin and mind but could not do so otherwise he would have been satisfied by uttering, smelling, seeing, hearing, touching or thinking of the food. Finally food was caught by *apan*, through the mouth.

Brahm entered through the cleft of the skull and man was born as *Jiv* (जीव), has three abodes (the eye, the mind and the heart) and three conditions of sleep (waking, dream and deep sleep). *Jiv* has three births — from his mother, on begetting a child (whom he nourishes as being part of himself) and by departing and leaving the body, to be re-born again; this cycle continues till he makes the effort to break it. So long as a man identifies himself with the body, he cannot escape the cycles of birth and death.

Brahm is Self, Indra, gods, person, and all creatures and beings which are supported by consciousness. Consciousness, knowledge, *pragya* is Brahm. Thus "*Pragyanam brahm*" (प्रज्ञानं ब्रह्म) or Brahm is the supreme knowledge. The *jiv*, on attainment of the knowledge, becomes one with the Supreme Self.

The Aitareya Upanishad enquires into the exact nature of the Self, and then answers:

Is it the Self by which we see, hear, smell, and taste,
Through which we speak in words? Is Self the mind
By which we perceive, direct, understand,
Know, remember, think, will, desire, and love?

These are but servants of the Self, who is
Pure consciousness. This Self is in all.[6]

---

[6]The Upanishads by Eknath Easwaran

Chhandogya Upanishad (Sam Ved)

The Chhandogya Upanishad (छान्दोग्योपनिषद्) of the Sam Ved is one of the longer and earlier Upanishads and comprises the last eight chapters of the ten-chapter Chhandogya Brahman. This Upanishad contains the doctrine of reincarnation as an ethical consequence of *karm*. It also lists and explains the value of human attributes such as speech, will, thought, meditation, understanding, strength, memory and hope.

The chief duties of man for the attainment of objects of the world / matters of life are the performance of actions (viz. rituals, sacrifices / *yagyas*), charity, austerity and sacred study, and the attainment of knowledge without which there can be no release. It is considered the best exponent of Brahm Vidya.

Five of the eight chapters deal with ritualistic worship or *upasana* (उपासना) with emphasis on meditation. The last three chapters discuss certain fundamental doctrines of the Vedant philosophy.

The first five chapters teach various meditations of Brahm under different names and forms which lead to knowledge and the supreme goal. The *vidyas* start with meditation on *Udgith* i.e. *Om* or *Pranav* where *Ud* is *pran*, heaven, sun, *sam* (ved); *Gi* is speech, sky, air, *yajur*; *Th* is food, earth, and fire, *Rik*. Thereafter various other meditations are covered.

Thus, in the first chapter of the Chhandogya Upanishad, the *upasanas* (prayers) which form part of the Sam Ved are given and discussions are on the essence and cause of all starting from earth to the Veds and *Udgith/Om*. Others covered are the various *prans* (*vyan, apan* etc. detailed in Prashna Upanishad).

In the second chapter, the meditations of Sam (Ved) / Sam ritual is discussed. It emphasizes the importance of chanting the sacred *Om*, and recommends a religious life, which constitutes rituals of worship or sacrifice, austerity, charity, and the study of the Veds, while living in the house of a guru.

In the third chapter, Madhuvidya—the meditation on Surya, the Gayatri *Upasana*, and the Shandilya (शांडिल्य) Vidya are all given. Shandilya was a great *rishi* who had the revelation of the Supreme Being, and *Vidya* is meditation, an art of thinking on the Supreme goal. This meditation begins with the proclamation of the all-comprehensiveness of Brahm: "*Sarvam khalvidam brahm* – All this is verily Brahm." Everything comes from That, everything is sustained in That, and everything returns to That[7]. That which is the origin, the sustenance and the dissolution of all things is Brahm. It is the cause of all things and every effect in the form of this creation is contained there.

The fourth chapter has the story of a grandson of Janashruti who was pious and generous. He learns of the existence of a

---

[7] http://www.swami-krishnananda.org/

reputed person known as 'Raikwa with the cart'. The grandson traces him, makes offerings to him and seeks knowledge of the deity that Raikwa worshipped. Raikwa then explains about the Samvarg (संवर्ग) Vidya - meditation on the all-absorbing Being. Samvarg implies that which sucks everything into itself or into which everything enters - the absorbent. Thereafter, through other guru-disciple discourses, knowledge of Brahm is then imparted.

In the fifth chapter, three Vidyas are elaborated - meditation on *pran, panchagni* (where libations or offerings are made **of** faith, *Som*, rain, food and seed — which creates the man) and the *Vaishvanar* (वैश्वानर) Self (where libations or offerings are made **to** *pran, vyan, apan, saman* and *udan*).

Panchagni-Vidya covers the knowledge of the five fires (the world, the god of rain, earth, man and woman), leading to the results of the offerings made to them viz. *som*, rain, food, semen and foetus. The chapter then discusses the various processes of manifestation or evolution, one's bondage and the way in which the cycle of transmigration revolves. *Sansar-chakra* is the continuously revolving wheel of life after life. There is a coming and going, descending and ascending. *Panchagni-Vidya* is a particular type of knowledge, or meditation, which is introduced to know the inner meaning of the common phenomenon of birth and death.

On *Vaishvanar*, the universal Self, the Upanishad states the mind is accustomed to think of only finite objects, and further to think of the *Atma* as an object, as if it is outside. The *Atma* is not external - the Self cannot be outside itself, it cannot be an object of itself, it cannot think itself, meditate upon itself as another, it cannot be other than itself. The *Vaishvanar-Atma*, the All-Self extends from the earth to the heavens, from the topmost level of manifestation to the lowest level.

There are two paths for man to go after death. Those who are the followers of Brahm knowledge and follow faith go by the godly path - the path of the *devs* and attain Brahm, they do not return to the world again. Those who perform rituals, sacrifices, undertake works of public utility and give alms, go to the *pitri* path and attain the world of the moon. After enjoying the fruits of their actions, they return to the world again by the same path as they went.

The evil doers go to hell and are punished for their misdeeds; they then attain the evil birth of beasts and insects etc. Those whose conduct here on earth has been good will quickly attain birth as a human in a worthy family. But those who do not practice meditation or perform rituals, nor are they evil-doers, do not follow either of these ways, they are born as insignificant creatures of repeated births and deaths – they die and they are born – a course that should be despised.

Chapter six describes the knowledge of Brahm as *Sat* ("*Ekam evadvitiyam*" - He is one only without a second), the cause of all beings; the later differ only in modification of names and forms.

Shvetaketu's father (Uddalaka also known as Aruni, son of Aruna) tells him that, one who neglects the study of the Veds, though born a Brahmin, can only be called *Brahm-bandhu* i.e. one who has Brahmins as his relatives. Shvetaketu then masters the four Veds, but becomes proud and pompous till he realises that his knowledge lacks depth. He seeks further knowledge from his father. Uddalaka explains that the knowledge of mud and of gold will give the knowledge of all pots and pans, as well as of all bracelets and necklaces. The mud and the gold are the truth and their modifications and transformations are temporary, mere name-forms. So too, the world, like the pot and the bracelet, is just an effect, the cause being *sat*. The *Atma* is *Sat*, the subtle essence of all.

Uddalaka's discourse then is on threefold development. The various types of organisms (those born from eggs, womb and roots) have originated on account of the mixture of the three elements (fire, water, earth) only, made possible on account of the substance of their bodies being provided by the three original elements. It then discusses the threefold nature – of the colour of fire, of food etc. Uddalaka then repeatedly tells Shvetaketu – **tatvamasi** – you are that. Some lines read:

> *As bees suck nectar from many a flower*
> *And make their honey one, so that no drop*
> *Can say, 'I am from this flower or that,'*
> *All creatures, though one, know not they are that*
> *One...*

Of everything he is the inmost Self.
He is the truth; he is the Self supreme.
You are that, Shvetaketu; you are that[8]. (tatvamasi)

Uddalaka says that rivers flow in all directions yet when they reach the sea, do not know which river they are. Similarly even though they do not know, all creatures have come from *Sat*. That which is the subtle essence (or the root of all), is the Self, that is the *Atma*, that is *Sat,* that is what you are Shvetaketu or **That thou art – *tatvamasi***

The *Jiv* is eternal and immortal but is born again and again as a transient mortal. He continues to accumulate *karm*, prompted by inherited impulses, and this activity produces consequences which he must shoulder. It is the body that decays and dies, not the *Jiv* or the Individualised Soul. A lump of salt dissolved in water disappears yet is present in every part of the water. So too *Sat,* though lost from view in the world, is still present in everything in the universe.

The *Jiv*, because of ignorance, is unable to recognise his Reality. A man left alone in the jungle discovers the way home when shown the direction by another. So also the *Jiv*, with the help of a teacher, reaches its real status, free from all the change and chance that is involved in the cycle of reincarnation – *Sansar* (संसार) - or the flow of time and space, of name and form.

---

[8] http://www.easwaran.org/

The seventh chapter has a discourse by Sanat Kumar to Narad. Narad says he knows the four Veds, the Itihas and the Purans, the knowledge of the rites, mathematics, knowledge of gods, of time, logic, ethics and politics, etymology, knowledge of the elements, war, astronomy etc., but still does not know Self. Sanat Kumar tells him that all that he studied is only a name and he should meditate upon the name as all names and forms represent Brahm.

Man may meditate on all names (being modifications of *Sat*) with varied results; the names in order of greatness and superiority are name, speech, mind, will, intelligence, meditation, knowledge, power, food, water, fire, *akash* or ether, remembrance, desire, and *Pran*. Knowledge of *pran* makes one a great speaker, yet the greatest speaker is one who knows *Sat* and speaks of *Sat*. It is Self alone which is below, above, behind, before, right, left – Self is all.

The eighth chapter says that in the city of Brahm is a secret dwelling, the lotus of the heart. Within this dwelling is a space and within that space is the fulfilment of our desires. What is within that space should be longed for and realized. As great as the infinite space beyond, is the space within the lotus of the heart. Both heaven and earth are contained in that inner space, as are fire and air, sun and moon, lightning and stars. Whether we know it in this world or do not know it, everything is contained in that inner space.[9]

---

[9] The Upanishads by Eknath Easwaran

It describes Brahm, and teaches that devotion leads to the attainment of all desires, that Self is without forms and qualities, and that the individual Self is the same as Brahm and *Atma*. The entire universe together with the earth and heaven, fire and air, sun and moon, lightening and stars etc. – whatever there is in this world and whatever is not, all is contained within the city of Brahm.

It then has another story. Both the demons (represented by Virochan), and the gods (represented by Indra), approached *Prajapati* to understand the Self as they were told that the Self is that which is to be known, to be sought after, which one must wish to know – the search of which all of the worlds and all the desires are obtained. After thirty two years of studentship, *Parajapati* told them that the Self is seen by the eye in the water or mirror (reflection). They saw themselves in the water, when they adorned themselves they saw the image was adorned too and when told by *Prajapati* that that was the Self, Brahm, they went away.

Prajapati saw them going and said that both were going away without having known and without having realized the Self; whoever of these, whether gods or demons, follow this doctrine would be destroyed.

The demon Virochan was satisfied with this doctrine and preached to the other demons that it was only by worshipping the Self, by attending the Self that one gains both the worlds – this as well as the other. But Indra (god), even before he reached the other *devtas* grasped that when the body was adorned or well-dressed the Self is adorned and well-dressed; when the body is blind or crippled or perishes the Self is also blind, crippled or perishes. He went back to *Prajapati* and after another thirty two years of studentship was told that he who moves about, and is attended upon in dreams that is the Self, the immortal and the fearless, Brahm.

Indra went away but was again dissatisfied. He realised that the dream Self is not blind when the body is blind nor is it affected by the faults of the body. Yet when the body is chased or harmed, the dream Self becomes conscious of pain and it sheds tears. After another thirty two years of studentship with *Prajapati*, Indra was told that when a man is asleep, with senses withdrawn and serene, and sees no dream—that is the Self, the immortal, fearless – Brahm.

Indra again went away satisfied in heart. But even before he had reached the gods, he saw the difficulty that the Self in dreamless sleep does not know itself as 'I am it'. It has therefore reached utter annihilation, as it were. Indra therefore did not see any good in this and went back to *Prajapati*.

This time he was asked to remain for five years after which *Prajapati* expounded that the body, which was mortal and held by death, was the abode of that immortal incorporeal (or disembodied) Self. The body is held by pleasure and pain but the Self, not being identified with the body, is untouched by them. Just as air, *akash* or ether, lightening etc. are without bodies and rise above, this serene being (Self) rises above the body and appears in its own form where he moves about laughing, playing and rejoicing, never thinking of the body into which he was born.

The Self is the one who sees, hears, smell and thinks through the organs of the eye, ear, nose and the mind (the divine eye). *Prajapati* said that he who knows that Self and understands It obtains all worlds and all desires. The Upanishad then says that the gods meditate on that Self, and therefore all the worlds belong to them.

The Upanishad concludes with mantras as prayer of a seeker of Eternal Life. It states that he who has studied the Veds at the house of a teacher, has settled down into a householder's life after leaving the teacher's house and continued the study of the Veds; who has withdrawn all the sense-organs into the Self; he who has not given pain to any creature—he who conducts himself thus, all through his life, reaches the World of Brahm after death and does not return.

(Note: Several of the shloks *in this Upanishad are common to the Brihadaranyak Upanishad. The philosophy and expressions in this Upanishad are also discussed in other Upanishads).*

Brihadaranyak Upanishad (Shukla Yajur Ved)

The Brihadaranyak Upanishad (बृहदारण्यक उपनिषद्) is one of the oldest and longest of the Upanishads (though some parts were reportedly composed after the Chhandogya Upanishad); it is contained within the Shatpath Brahman of the Shukla Yajur Ved. It has the same opening invocation as the Ish Upanishad viz. *Om purnamadah purnamidam .....*

It talks of Brahm, *Jiv* and *Jagat* and clearly shows that Brahm is the absolute unity or *advaitya*, identical with *Atma* or Self and the world is his manifestation. Brahm and Self are one and the same. *Jiv,* on being united with the body, becomes deluded and is subject to pleasure and pain, birth and death etc. But on obtaining knowledge, it attains its true nature and supreme form and then regards "*Aham brahmasmi*—I am Brahm", and "thou art the Self", the *Sat* and the inner Self of all. Brahm is of two-fold nature – *Sagun* and *Nirgun*. As *Sagun* or manifested he is the cause of all names, forms, beings and the world; as *Nirgun* (or unmanifested) he is without qualities, best described as *Neti Neti*.

The Brihadaranyak Upanishad, which is generally recognized to be the most important of the Upanishads, consists of three sections (*Kands*) of two chapters each. These *Kands* are *Madhu Kand, Muni* or *Yagvalkya Kand* and *Khil Kand.* The *Madhu Kand* (मधु काण्ड) expounds the teachings of the basic identity of the individual and the Universal Self, the *Muni* or Yagyavalkya *Kand* (मुनि काण्ड) provides the philosophical justification of the teaching, and the *Khil Kand* (खिल काण्ड) deals with certain modes of worship and meditation viz. *sravan* or hearing the teaching, *manan* or logical reflection, and *nidhidhyasan* or contemplative meditation.

The first chapter of the Madhu Kand treats the sacrificial horse as *Prajapati* - the creator of all, hunger and death, as also the destroyer of all; and *Udgith* as Brahm the supreme of all. *(Note: A little explanation here – the Ashvamedh yagya or the horse sacrifice was undertaken by princes and kings in ancient times for the purpose of name, fame etc., and to show their superiority. This chapter gives a more profound meaning — it contemplates the universe as a sacrificial horse and covers the creation of the universe.)*

Brahm alone existed at first and he created the world and food for all. The Upanishad discusses the superiority of the vital force (*pran*) amongst all functions represented by the sense organs. This is explained through a battle on the singing of *Udgith* between the divine forces or gods / *Devs* (representing people who are able to subdue their natural impulses) and the non-divine forces or demons / *Asurs*, (people who follow their natural inclinations).

There is then the story of creation; there was One alone without a second - the universal cause of everything - that began to contemplate, this was the beginning of the Will to create. It felt that it was alone, willed to be other than itself, split itself into two and became the cause of further divisions.

Despite this multiplicity and duality, apparently becoming 'other' than itself, there is a unity among things, the cause remains as it was.

The Upanishad goes on to describe the classification, both of the gods in heaven and of the human beings. In the beginning was Brahm. He projected *kshatriyahood* — and the *kshatriyas* (rulers) among the gods: *Indra, Varun, Som* (Moon), *Rudra, Yam, Mrityu* (Death) and *Ishan*. There is none higher than the *Kshatriyas*, the brahmin sits below and worships the *kshatriya* at the *Rajasuya yagya* — the *yagya* conducted by a powerful king declaring himself emperor. Yet, at the end of it, the *kshatriya* king takes refuge in the brahmin.

Brahm then projected the *Vaishya* caste - those classes of gods who are designated in groups: the *Vasus, Rudras, Adityas, Vishwadevs* and *Maruts*. He projected the *shudra* caste — *Pushan* - the earth (the nourisher); for it nourishes all that exists. He further projected that excellent form of righteousness (Dharm), which is the controller of the *kshatriya*, and even a weak man can defeat a stronger man through the strength of righteousness.

It is further pointed out that every action and every effort is finally useless and futile if it is bereft of the consciousness of the *Atma.* It explains fear as being due to duality and coming from someone else — if there is no 'anotherness', there is no fear. The Upanishad mentions that creation began in a particular fashion, in an ordered form. The celestials were created (first *Agni*, *Indra*, *Vasu* and *Pushan*), simultaneously with human beings; then the plants and the five elements – *akash* or ether, air, fire, water, earth. Every deity has been projected from one or the other limb of the *Virat Purush*.

Prajapati's production of the world as food for himself is then discussed—food, or a diet of the senses – the object of desire. Anything that is perceived, sensed and thought through the mind is food therefor. All objects of desire are the food of the senses and the mind. The whole manifested world is the food of consciousness, thus *Prakriti* is the 'food' of *Purush.* The Supreme Being created food for the Spirit - this vast world of creation.

The second chapter (which is also the Madhu Kand) deals with the discourse of Balaki and Ajatshatru that Brahm is not limited and defined but all-pervading and infinite. Balaki meditated on Brahm as sun, moon, lightning, akash or ether, air, fire or water etc. Ajatshatru said Brahm should instead be mediated upon as surpassing all men, the head of everything; radiant and resplendent *Som*, illuminating, full and stable, irresistible, victorious and unconquerable, forbearing and agreeable, shining, as life etc. Finally Balaki, a Brahmin, seeks knowledge from the kshatriya king Ajatshatru who also talks of the presence of a person when in sleep and in deep sleep.

It describes the meditation of Brahm as *Sagun* or *Nirgun* - manifested and unmanifested. It also teaches *Madhu Vidya,* that the Self is the essence of all, and therefore should be known and worshipped by all. It discusses the interdependence of created objects, where earth, water, truth, mankind, *dharm* etc. are all the honey of all beings, and all beings are the honey of this earth, water, etc. *(Note: Madhu or honey is the composite fruit of numerous actions, nectar is the essence of many flowers, and honey has been interpreted by different sources as to mean effect or essence or bliss).*

Similarly, the bright, immortal being that is in this earth and the bright, immortal, worldly being that is in the body are both honey. These are nothing but the Self. The knowledge of this Self is the means to immortality; this underlying unity is Brahm; this knowledge of Brahm is the means of becoming all.

This *Kand* also describes a number of meditations – *purush*, death, *udgith*, *antaryami* and *madhu*. It has the famous mantra **Asto ma sadgamaya, tamso ma jyotirgamaya, mrityorma amritam gamaya** (असतो मा सद्गमय । तमसो मा ज्योतिर्गमय । मृत्योर्मा अमृतं गमय ।) Or *"From the unreal lead me to the real, From darkness lead me to light, From death lead me to immortality!"*

Chapter III which is the first part of the *Muni Kand* is the discourse of Yagyavalkya and learned Brahmans in the assembly of King Janak about certain prayers and rituals / sacrifices, the *hotri, adhvaryu, udgatri,* and the *Brahman* priests.

It starts with the story of King Janak who has a gathering of priests and scholars and wishes to know which of them was the most erudite. He decorated with gold, the horns of a thousand cows and said these could be driven home by the best Vedic scholar amongst them. None of the Brahmins dared do so but Yagyavalkya asked his students to drive home the cows. This (apparent arrogance of Yagyavalkya) infuriated the other *rishis*. Yagyavalkya said that he bowed to the best Vedic scholar, but just wished to have the cows.

Thereafter one after another several *rishis* questioned him and Yagyavalkya's answers form a major part of the *Muni Kand* which teaches the highest knowledge of Brahm for the attainment of liberation, the supreme goal.

It discusses the eight organs and their eight objects viz. nose - smell, speech - name, tongue - taste, eye - form/colour, ear - sound, mind - desire, hands – work, and skin – touch. The Self that is within all is that which breathes through the *pran*, moves downward through the *apan*, pervades through the *vyan* and which goes out with the *udan*. It is that which is free of hunger and thirst, grief, delusion, old age and death.

The Self, the Inner Controller is Immortal, it inhabits the earth yet is within it, the earth does not know it but its body is the earth, and it controls the earth from within. Similar expressions are then given for water, fire, sky, air, heaven, sun, the quarters of space, the moon and the stars, *akash* or ether, darkness and light, and finally of all beings.

The Upanishad then explains similarly with reference to the body – the nose (*pran*) and of the organs of speech, the eye, the ear, the mind, skin, intellect, and the organ of generation. He is never seen, but is the Seer; He is never heard, but is the Hearer; He is never thought of, but is the Thinker; He is never known, but is the Knower.

In the discourse with Gargi, a renowned women philosopher, Yagyavalkya said that which is above heaven and below the earth, within which is this heaven and earth, which is past, present and future and by which this is woven and cross-woven is the unmanifested *akash* or ether, which in turn is pervaded by *Akshar* (or Brahm / *Atma*). It is neither gross nor subtle, neither short nor long, neither red nor moist; It is neither shadow nor darkness, neither air nor ether; It is unattached, without taste or smell, without eyes or ears, without tongue or mind; It is non-effulgent, without vital breath or mouth, without measure and without exterior or interior. It does not eat anything, nor is it eaten by anyone. Under It, the sun and moon, heaven and earth, moments, periods, days and nights, fortnights, months, seasons and years are held in their respective positions, and rivers flow in their directions.

In response to another question, Yagyavalka gives the number of gods in various ways. He says there are thirty-three gods; the others are but manifestations of them. These gods are the eight *Vasus,* the eleven *Rudras,* the twelve *Adityas,* and Indra and Prajapati.

The eight *Vasus* are fire, earth, air, sky, sun, heaven, moon and the stars - called the *Vasus* for in them this entire universe is placed. The eleven *Rudras* are the ten organs in the human body viz. the five sensory organs or *gyanendriyas*, the five organs of action or *karmendriyas*, and the mind (so called because when they depart from this mortal body, they make one's relatives weep). The twelve *Adityas* are the twelve Sun-gods and offspring of Aditi - a different Aditya shining in each month of the year.

He then says that there are six gods—fire, the earth, the air, the sky, the sun and heaven for these six comprise all those. The three gods are the three worlds, because all those gods are comprised in these three. The two gods are matter and the vital breath (*pran*). The one God is the vital breath (Hiranyagarbh); it is Brahm, which is called That.

Chapter IV contains the teaching of Yagyavalkya to Janak about Brahm knowledge and how to attain liberation. Man goes about with the help of light but when the sun has set, the moon has set, the fire has gone out and even speech (sound) has stopped, it is the Self that serves as light with which he sits, goes out, works and returns. He then discusses the Self as *purush,* identified with the intellect, and which is in the midst of the organs. When born, a person (the individual Self) assumes a body, is joined with evils and when he dies he discards those evils.

It also describes the states of waking, dream, deep sleep and

Turiya and how the Self is united with senses, mind and *pran*, and acts and conducts itself in these states. There are only two states: the one in this world and the other in the next world. The third, the intermediate, is the dream state. When a person is in that intermediate state, he surveys both states: the one here in this world and the other in the next world and sees both evils (sufferings) and joys.

There are no real chariots in that (dream) state, no animals to be yoked to them, no roads there, but he creates the chariots, the animals and the roads. There are no pleasures in that state, no joys and no rejoicings, but he creates the pleasures, joys and rejoicings. There are no pools in that state, no reservoirs, no rivers, but he creates the pools, reservoirs and rivers. He indeed is the agent who travels alone, makes the body insensible in sleep but himself remains awake and watches those which lie dormant.

Purush remains unaffected by whatever he sees in the dream state, for this infinite being is unattached. The subtle body is the storehouse of impressions. When he feels as if he were being killed or being chased by an elephant - when he fancies, thorough ignorance, whatever frightful thing he has experienced in the waking state, that is the dream state.

In deep sleep he is free from desires, evils, fear; this infinite being (the Self), fully embraced by the Supreme Self, knows nothing that is within or without. That indeed is his form, in which all his desires are fulfilled, in which all desires become the Self and which is free from desires and devoid of grief. In this state a father is no more a father, a mother is no more a mother, the worlds are no more the worlds, the Veds are no more the Veds; this form of his is untouched by either good or evil deeds, beyond all the woes of his heart. In deep sleep it becomes transparent like water, the witness, one without a second. This is the World of Brahm, its supreme attainment; this is its supreme bliss.

On Death and the hereafter, Yagyavalkya says that just as a leech moving on a blade of grass reaches its end, takes hold of another and draws itself together towards it, so does the Self, after throwing off this body, fashion another, a newer and better, form.

Because of attachment, the transmigrating Self, together with its work, attains that result to which it's subtle body or mind clings. Having exhausted in the other world, the results of whatever work it did in this life, it returns from that world to this world for fresh work. But the man who does not desire—who is freed from desire, whose only object of desire is the Self, being Brahm, he merges in Brahm. When all the desires that dwell in his heart are got rid of, the mortal man becomes immortal and attains Brahm in this very body. The Self is free from taint, beyond the *akash* or ether, birthless, infinite and unchanging.

It is the controller of all, the lord of all, the ruler of all. It does not become greater through good deeds or smaller through evil deeds. This Self is That which has been described as Not this, not this (*Neti Neti*). It is imperceptible, undecaying, unattached, unfettered. He further says that as expressed by a Rig verse: '*This is the eternal glory of Brahm: It neither increases nor decreases through work. Therefore one should know the nature of That alone. Knowing It one is not touched by evil action.*'[10] He who knows It as such becomes Self—controlled, calm, withdrawn into himself, patient and collected; he sees the Self in his own Self (body); he sees all as the Self. He becomes sinless, taintless, and free from doubts. That great, unborn Self is undecaying, immortal, undying and fearless; It is Brahm (infinite).

It also has (twice) his teaching to his wife Maitreyi (who prefers knowledge to a share of his worldly possessions). Yagyavalkya explains that it is not for the sake of the husband that the husband is loved; he is loved for the sake of the Self which, in its true nature, is one with the Supreme Self. Similarly the wife, sons, wealth, animals, etc. or gods, the Veds, all the world are loved for the sake of the Self. It is the Self that should be realized—should be heard of, reflected on and meditated upon. By the realisation of the Self through hearing, reflection and meditation, all this is known.

As a lump of salt has neither inside nor outside and is altogether a homogeneous mass of taste, Self too has neither inside nor outside and is a homogeneous mass of

---

[10] swamij.com

Intelligence. When there is duality then one sees another, smells or tastes or speaks to, hears or knows another. But when to the knower of Brahm everything has become the Self, then what should he see and through what, what should he smell, taste, speak to, hear, touch and through what.

The *Khil Kand* is the last two chapters which describe certain teachings for attainment of knowledge and the supreme goal. It advocates the practicing of control or restraint, donation or charity and compassion or mercy. It teaches the knowledge and meditation of Brahm under the names of *satya*, heart, mind, lightening, the Veds, the *Vaisvanar* fire, food, *pran*, Gayatri.

The superiority of the vital force (*pran*) amongst all functions represented by the sense organs are again discussed – this time by showing that the body can live without one or the other sense organs but not without *pran*. It also discusses conception and birth as religious rites and has passages which discuss aspects of sex mantras related to progeny etc. The knowledge of *pran*, *panchgani* fire, as given in the Chhandogya Upanishad is also found here.

The crux of the Upanishads is that *moksh* can be achieved by meditating with the awareness that one's *Atma* is one with all things, and that 'one' is Brahm, which becomes the 'all'.

Mahavakyas

The Upanishads also contain *Mahavakyas* (महावाक्य) or aphorisms or maxims. Some of these are:

1. *"Pragyanam brahm"* (प्रज्ञानं ब्रह्म) or Brahm is the supreme knowledge or Consciousness is Brahm (from the Aitareya Upanishad of the Rig Ved).
2. *"Aham brahmasmi"* (अहं ब्रह्मास्मि) or I am Brahm (from the Brihadaranyak Upanishad of the Yajur Ved).
3. *"Tat tva masi"* (तत्त्वमसि) or That is what you are (from the Chhandogya Upanishad of the Sam Ved).
4. *"Ayam atma brahm"* (अयम् आत्मा ब्रह्म) or I am this Self (Atma) that is Brahm (from the Mandukya Upanishad of the Atharva Ved, and also from the Brihadaranyak Upanishad of the Yajur Ved).
5. *"Ekam evadvitiyam"* (एकमेवाद्वितीयम्) or He is One only without a second (from the Chhandogya Upanishad).
6. *"Sarvam khalvidam brahm"* (सर्वं खल्विदं ब्रह्म) or All is truly Brahm, is also from the Chhandogya Upanishad.

Another important saying though not from the Upanishad is *"Brahma satyam jagat mithya"* or Brahm is real; the world is unreal (from Vivekchudamani ascribed to Adi Shankaracharya).

Some extracts

The Nasidiya Sukt (Rig Ved)

The Nasadiya Sukt (*na asat* "not the non-existent") also known as the Hymn of Creation is the 129th hymn of the 10th Mandal of the Rigved (10:129). It is concerned with cosmology and the origin of the universe.

Then even nothingness was not, nor existence,
There was no air then, nor the heavens beyond it.
What covered it? Where was it? In whose keeping
Was there then cosmic water, in depths unfathomed?

Then there was neither death nor immortality
nor was there then the torch of night and day.
The One breathed windlessly and self-sustaining.
There was that One then, and there was no other.

At first there was only darkness wrapped in darkness.
All this was only unillumined water.
That One which came to be, enclosed in nothing,
arose at last, born of the power of heat.

In the beginning desire descended on it -
that was the primal seed, born of the mind.
The sages who have searched their hearts with wisdom
know that which is is kin to that which is not.

And they have stretched their cord across the void,
and know what was above, and what below.
Seminal powers made fertile mighty forces.
Below was strength, and over it was impulse.

But, after all, who knows, and who can say
Whence it all came, and how creation happened?
the gods themselves are later than creation,
so who knows truly whence it has arisen?

Whence all creation had its origin,
he, whether he fashioned it or whether he did not,
he, who surveys it all from highest heaven,
he knows - or maybe even he does not know.[11]

Atma (Kath Upanishad)

The following lines are extracted from the *Kath* Upanishad.

That whence the sun's orb rises up,
And that in which it sinks again:
In it the gods are all contained,
Beyond it none can ever pass

Its form can never be to sight apparent,
Not any one may with his eye behold it:
By heart and mind and soul alone they grasp it,
And those who know it thus become immortal

Since not by speech and not by thought,
Not by the eye can it be reached:
How else may it be understood
But only when one says "it is"?[12]

---

[11] Translation by RT Griffith
[12] A history of Sanskrit Literature by Arthur A Macdonell

Sources

In the preparation of this book, I have consulted a large number of sources. Translations of the Ved Sanhitas that I have gone through, at least in part, are by RT Griffith, AB Keith and M Bloomfield. A history of Sanskrit Literature by Arthur A Macdonell gives a great understanding of the Veds. Some of the sites frequently visited are: esamskriti.com, sanskritweb.net, ancientvoice.wikidot.com, hindupedia.com, britannica.com, bbc.co.uk/ and hinduonline.co/index.html.

Some of the books seen are Ancient Indian History and Civilization by Sailendra Nath Sen, Indian Philosophy by S. Radhakrishnan, Hindu Culture – An Introduction by Swami Tejomayananda. For the Darshans, I particularly liked justforkidsonly.com. A conceptual explanation on the four Veds, and on *Sat* and *Asat,* is seen at www.swami-krishnananda.org.

I have read Hindi or English translations of the Ramcharitmanas, the Bhagvad Gita, the Srimad Bhagvat Puran, the Shiv Puran, a 365 pages summarized commentary of Yog Vashishth, the Vivekchudamani, the Durga Saptsashi and the Astavakra Gita. I have also gone through, in part, Valmiki's Ramayan, the Garud Puran and some of the Upanishads besides the entire ten Upanishads covered here.

The basic book that I have used for the Upanishads is "Prasthanik-Tryi or The Three-fold Vedant" by Shri R C Vidyarthi (a book gifted by the author to my grandfather).

Straight English translations have also been read at swamij.com, sacred-texts.com, sankaracharya.org/, bharatadesam.com/, estudantedavedanta.net/ and the book "Penguin Classics - The Upanishads".

For detailed commentaries on the individual Upanishads, the simplest and best I have found are those by T.N.Sethumadhavan at esamskriti.com. Excellent philosophical explanations were found on swami-krishnananda.org. Another is The Upanishads by Swami Nikhilananda.

www.kavitakosh.org has beautiful poetic Hindi translations of the Upanishads by Mridul Kirti.

And of course the mother of all sources, Wikipedia, has been repeatedly sourced – I cannot thank them enough.

www.ingramcontent.com/pod-product-compliance
Lightning Source LLC
LaVergne TN
LVHW051223200726
843510LV00011B/1461